The Best Web Sites for Teachers

Third Edition

Richard M. Sharp
Vicki F. Sharp
Martin G. Levine

© International Society for Technology in Education, Third Edition, 2000

Director of Publishing
Jean Marie Hall

Project Coordinator
Corinne Tan

Editor
Christy McMannis, The Electronic Page

Editorial Assistants
Tyler Long
Jacklyn Arvin

Production
Corinne Tan

Book Design
Corinne Tan

Cover Design
Signe Landin

Administrative Office
1787 Agate Street
Eugene, OR 97403-1923
Phone: 541.346.4414
Fax: 541.346.5890
E-Mail: iste@oregon.uoregon.edu

Customer Service Office
480 Charnelton Street
Eugene, OR 97401-2626
Order Desk: 800.336.5191
Order Fax: 541.302.3778
E-Mail: cust_svc@iste.org

World Wide Web: www.iste.org

Third Edition
ISBN 1-56484-160-X

From the Publisher

The International Society for Technology in Education (ISTE) promotes appropriate uses of technology to support and improve learning, teaching, and administration. As part of that mission, ISTE's goal is to provide individuals and organizations with high-quality and timely information, materials, and services that support technology in education.

Our Books and Courseware Department works with educators to develop and produce classroom-tested materials and resources that support ISTE's mission. We look for content that emphasizes the use of technology where it can make a difference—making the teacher's job easier; saving time; motivating students; helping students with various learning styles, abilities, or backgrounds; and creating learning environments that are new and unique or that would be impossible without technology.

We develop products for students, classroom teachers, lab teachers, technology coordinators, and teacher educators, as well as for parents, administrators, policy makers, and visionaries. All of us face the challenge of keeping up with new technologies and the research about their educational applications while we are learning about and implementing appropriate applications in our teaching/learning situations. Please help us in our efforts to help you by providing feedback about this book and other ISTE products and by giving us your suggestions for further development.

Jean Marie Hall, Director of Publishing
Phone: 541.346.2519; E-Mail: jhall@iste.org

Anita Best, Acquisitions Editor
Phone: 541.346.2400; E-Mail: abest@iste.org

International Society for Technology in Education
Books and Courseware Department
1787 Agate Street
Eugene, OR 97403-1923

About the Authors

Dr. Richard M. Sharp, professor of elementary education at California State University, Northridge, is the author of numerous books and articles on topics related to mathematics. His most recent books include *WebDoctor* (Quality Medical Book-St. Martin Distributor, 1998), *The Best Web Sites for Teachers, First and Second editions* (International Society for Technology in Education, 1996, 1998), *The Best Math and Science Web Sites for Teachers* (International Society for Technology in Education, 1997), *Scribble Scrabble and Other Ready-in-a-Minute Math Games* (McGraw-Hill, 1995), and *The Sneaky Square & Other Math Activities* (McGraw-Hill, 1996). He serves as a computer consultant and trainer for software publishers and school districts in Southern California. He currently writes a medical column for Health Scout. He has coauthored a Web page entitled "Web Sites and Resources for Teachers," which covers all curriculum areas. The URL is www.csun.edu/~vceed009/.

Dr. Vicki F. Sharp, professor of elementary education at California State University, Northridge, is the author of numerous books and articles on topics related to the use of computers in education. Her most recent books include *PowerPoint 98 In One Hour—Macintosh Version* and *PowerPoint 97 In One Hour—Windows Version* (International Society for Technology in Education, 1999), *The Best Web Sites for Teachers, First and Second editions* (International Society for Technology in Education, 1996, 1998), *HyperStudio 3.1/3.0 In One Hour—Windows* (International Society for Technology in Education, 1998), *WebDoctor* (Quality Medical Book-St. Martin Distributor, 1998), *Computer Education for Teachers, Third Edition* (McGraw-Hill, Fall 1998), *HyperStudio 3.1 In One Hour—Macintosh* (International Society for Technology in Education, 1997), *Netscape Navigator 3.0 In One Hour* (International Society for Technology in Education, 1997), *The Best Math and Science Web Sites for Teachers* (International Society for Technology in Education, 1997), *Internet Guide for Education* (Wadsworth, 1996), and *Scribble Scrabble and Other Ready-in-a-Minute Math Games* (McGraw-Hill, 1995). She frequently writes about children's software for magazines and serves as a computer consultant and trainer for software publishers and school districts in Southern California. With her husband Dr. Richard M. Sharp, she maintains a Web site covering all curriculum areas. The URL is www.csun.edu/~vceed009/.

Dr. Martin G. Levine teaches courses in methods of teaching social studies, ESL, and bilingual education at California State University, Northridge. He holds the Bilingual Certificate of Competence and the General Secondary Credential awarded by the State of California. He has taught social studies and English at the secondary level and has published articles in social studies and foreign language journals for teachers. He has coauthored *The Best Web Sites for Teachers, First and Second editions* (International Society for Technology in Education, 1996, 1998) and *The Best Math and Science Web Sites for Teachers* (International Society for Technology in Education, 1997). He has authored numerous Web pages covering such topics as foreign language instruction, ESL, and social studies. The type of content and URLs for these pages are: Lesson Plans and Resources for ESL and Bilingual Teachers (www.csun.edu/~hcedu013/eslindex.html), Foreign Language Study Abroad (www.csun.edu/~hcedu013/LanguageAbroad.html), and Lesson Plans and Resources for Social Studies Teachers (www.csun.edu/~hcedu013/index.html).

Acknowledgments

We wish to thank to Anita Best, Jean Hall, Corinne Tan, and Christy McMannis for their excellent editorial work, advice, and invaluable assistance and direction. Thanks to Judi Mathis Johnson at the International Society for Technology in Education (ISTE) and Susan Dahl at the Fermi National Accelerator Laboratory Lederman Science Center-IRC for their development work on the ISTE forms for evaluating new and recommended Web sites. Thanks also goes to Corinne Tan for her conscientiousness, skill, and diligence in preparing this book for publication; Tyler Long and Jacky Arvin for their assistance in verifying the existence of all the sites listed in the book; and Signe Landin for the wonderful cover she created.

Thanks to Dave Pola, creative marketing director of Equilibrium, for DeBabelizer, a real time saver. DeBabelizer was used to batch produce the screenshots and enhance the images. You can reach Equilibrium by phone at 415.332.4343 or on the Web at www. equilibrium.com/.

Richard and Vicki Sharp offer a very special thanks to their son, David Sharp, for his help.

This book is dedicated to Vicki Sharp's parents, Bobbie E. Friedman and the late Paul J. Friedman.

Richard M. Sharp
Vicki F. Sharp
Martin G. Levine
California State University, Northridge

Visit ISTE Online

www.iste.org

Like technology itself, ISTE's online support of technology-using educators is a process of constant growth and change rather than a static presence. At any given time, new features are being added and current offerings are being expanded and improved. As this book goes to press, **www.iste.org** supports the effective use of technology in K–12 teaching and learning within the following broad categories:

Technology Standards
Current educational technology standards for K–12 student and teacher education to download free or purchase in print form

ISTE Online Bookstore
Selected ed-tech books and products with online ordering and membership discount options

Learning & Leading with Technology
Feature and curriculum-area articles from ISTE's highly regarded, flagship publication

ISTE Update
Membership newsletter with the latest ISTE and general ed-tech news and events

Teacher Resources
Categorized links to Web sites providing support and materials for educators and students

Discussion Groups
A cyberplace for ISTE members to make connections and share perspectives

Professional Development Services
Online conference information, registration, and submissions

Research Projects
Recent research that's likely to affect classrooms, teachers, and teacher education

Member Services
ISTE memberships, organization affiliates, and subscriptions to publications

A copy of the *ISTE Catalog* can be ordered online, one of the many products, tools, and services that ISTE offers online at no cost to its members, customers, and other online visitors.

Table of Contents

Introduction

New to the Third Edition

The third edition of *The Best Web Sites for Teachers* contains a number of additions and changes to the second edition that result from changes occurring on the World Wide Web. The third edition includes the following:

- ⚙ more sites offering lesson plans

- ⚙ descriptions of 25% new sites

- ⚙ deletion of sites no longer in existence

- ⚙ updated links for all sites

- ⚙ a revised Getting Started section for Internet Explorer and Netscape Communicator

- ⚙ a revised Tips for using Netscape Communicator and Internet Explorer

- ⚙ a revised Tips for Finding Inaccessible URLs

- ⚙ additional information on search engines

The Internet and the World Wide Web: What Are They?

Currently, the terms *Internet* and *World Wide Web* permeate every facet of our lives. Everywhere we travel we hear people talking about worldwide communication using the Internet. We see it in print in magazines and newspapers and hear it discussed on television, on talk radio, and in educational circles.

The Internet is a huge, worldwide network of connected computer networks with no single, master control-center or authority. The Internet was created for military research purposes in 1969 by the U.S. Department of Defense, whose major concern was to ensure mass communication of information and at the same time provide maximum security. Although the Internet has been in existence a long time, until recently it has been very difficult for the general public to access it. Because of this difficulty, only scientists and academics used it. It wasn't until 1989 with the development of the World Wide Web that the general public became heavy users of the Internet.

The World Wide Web is an easy way to navigate the Internet. The Web incorporates text, graphics, and sounds in electronic documents called *home pages* or *Web sites*. Each home page or Web site has its own unique URL, or address. (URL stands for Uniform Resource Locator.)

Certain items on Web pages are underlined. These underlined items are called *links*. The World Wide Web gets its name from these links because they are like threads in a spider's web. By clicking the link with the mouse, you can jump from one page on the Web to another, be it a page on the same computer or a page on another computer on the other side of the world. One document is linked to another, which is linked to another, and so on.

What's on the World Wide Web for Teachers?

There are thousands of useful Web sites for teachers that take advantage of the Web's multimedia capabilities. You can visit a museum, take a lesson in a foreign language, play a math game, explore the human brain, read interactive stories, participate in online polls and discussion groups, listen to music, and download lesson plans.

How Can I Find Things on the World Wide Web?

The World Wide Web provides you with tools to search for resources. These search tools bear names, such as Infind.com, Infoseek, AltaVista, Yahoo!, Deja News, Excite, Ask Jeeves, Snap.com, and About.com. (See Appendix 2 for Web site information on various search tools.) You enter keywords to find lists of sites that may contain the information you are looking for. Another way to find information on the Web is to know the address (the URL) for a site. All Web URLs start with http://. For example, to connect to the home page of the White House, you would type http://www.whitehouse.gov/.

How Do I Access the World Wide Web?

To access the Web, you need a connection to the Internet, which you can get through a commercial Internet Service Provider (ISP). Two popular ones are America Online (800.827.6364), and EarthLink (800.395.8410). Online services providers usually charge a monthly fee less than $20 for unlimited Internet access. If you already have access to the Internet, you can find a list of ISPs using *The List* at http://thelist.internet.com/.

Another place to find information is in your local Yellow Pages or from a local computer user group.

What Kind of Computer Hardware and Software Do I Need?

To access the Web effectively, you need a computer running MS-DOS or Windows with at least a 386 processor and 8 MB (megabytes) of RAM, or a Macintosh computer running System 7.0 or higher with at least 8 MB of memory. You will also need a modem. If possible, use a modem with a transfer speed of 56K. A 28.8-bps modem will work, but it will operate at a much slower speed.

What Is the Purpose of This Book?

The authors have searched the Internet and World Wide Web and identified more than 700 sites across the K–12 curriculum that we feel will benefit busy teachers who may not have time to carry out lengthy searches themselves. We believe that this collection of sites will provide teachers with a good starting place for Internet exploration on their own. Be forewarned that Internet resources come and go. There is no guarantee that all of the sites included in this book will be accessible when you try to open them. You might find that the problem is temporary, or that the resource simply may have moved to a different address, or that the site has disappeared. If your initial effort to visit a specific Web site fails, try again later. Because Web sites are frequently redesigned to take advantage of the latest developments in Web technology, you may find that some of the graphical displays of Web pages in this book will be different from what you see on your monitor when you access the site.

How Is This Book Organized?

The Web sites in this book are organized alphabetically by the following K-12 subject areas: art, bilingual education, drama, ESL, foreign language, health education/physical education, journalism, language arts, math, multicultural, multisubjects, music, science, social studies, special education, and vocational/technical education. Within each subject area, the sites are organized into at least one of three categories: lesson plans, other resources, and exhibits and museums.

In addition, Appendix 1 describes Web sites for discussion groups, called *newsgroups*, that allow teachers to read and post messages. These groups are similar to electronic bulletin boards. Appendix 1 also describes mailing lists, or *listservs*, through which teachers can subscribe to electronic newsletters. Appendix 2 lists Web sites for information on search tools. Appendix 3 provides some sample forms for evaluating recommended and new Web sites. The Web sites mentioned in this book are indexed both alphabetically by title and alphabetically by title within each subject-area category.

What's Included in the Descriptions of Sites?

The sites described for each subject area may include a wide range of material—lesson plans and pictures that can be printed, online multimedia presentations for students, interactive games, weekly brain teasers, searchable activities, databases for teachers, contests, pen pal opportunities, forms, downloadable graphics, videos, and many other resources that can enrich the K-12 curriculum. The descriptions of the sites usually indicate whether the sites are for teachers or students, as well as the grade levels for which the site material is intended.

What Were the Criteria for Selecting the Sites?

Because anyone with access to the Web can rather easily establish a Web site, there are many so-called educational Web sites that contain very little useful information, even though they may be very visually appealing. Furthermore, many sites with good information contain graphics that take too long to download to your computer and therefore tax the attention span of both adults and students who are accustomed to fast-paced forms of media. Many sites are poorly constructed with hard-to-read screens, inactive or missing links, and distracting graphics. In selecting sites to include in this book, we considered how appropriate, relevant, and useful the sites would be for teaching and enhancing the K-12 curriculum. We have selected sites that, in general, fulfill the following criteria:

- The site contains appropriate, relevant, and timely information.

- The site is organized effectively on a stable Internet location with good connectivity so that teachers and students can easily find the information they are seeking.

- The site can be downloaded in a reasonable period of time.

- The site is updated regularly.

- The site is an award winner that has been cited for having valuable, authoritative, and reliable information.

The two evaluation forms in Appendix 3 offer some criteria to help you evaluate educational Web sites on your own. The first form, Educational Web Sites Recommended by Others, will help you evaluate sites described in this book for use in your own classroom. The second form, Educational Web Sites You Discover, will help you evaluate new sites you encounter in your Web travels.

Keep Us Up to Date

We hope that this book will enrich your Webbing experience, which will translate into more productive time on the Internet. If you have comments or wish to add some of your favorite Web sites to the next edition, please let us know. The e-mail address is vicki.sharp@csun.edu.

Getting Started With Your Browser

To take advantage of the Web, you need a software program called a *browser*. All Web pages displayed in this book can be opened using either Microsoft Internet Explorer or Netscape Communicator. They both work in a similar way, although the display of the home page on your monitor may look different. The following instructions tell you how to enter a URL to display a home page.

Netscape Communicator

After you launch Netscape Navigator, you will see a toolbar at the top of its window. The toolbar has commands, such as Print, Home, and Back.

Now follow these steps.

1. If you are using Netscape Communicator 4.5, from the **File** menu, point to **Open** then choose **Location in Navigator** (⌘-O)

*Note: Click **Open** on the toolbar for Netscape 3.0.*

2. Type the following URL in the Location dialog box:
    http://www.csun.edu/~vceed009/

3. Click the Open button.

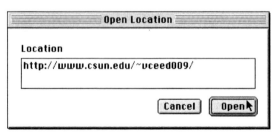

Internet Explorer

After launching Internet Explorer, you will see a toolbar with commands, such as Stop, Back, and Forward.

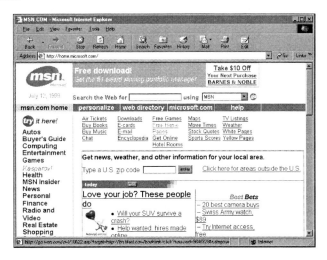

Now follow these steps.

1. From the **File** menu, click **Open** (Ctrl + O).

2. Type the following URL in the Open dialog box:
   http://www.csun.edu/~vceed009/

3. Click the OK button.

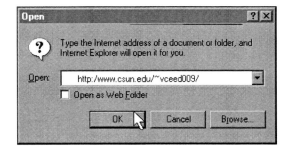

Netscape Communicator and Internet Explorer

4. After a few seconds, the home page corresponding to the URL will appear.

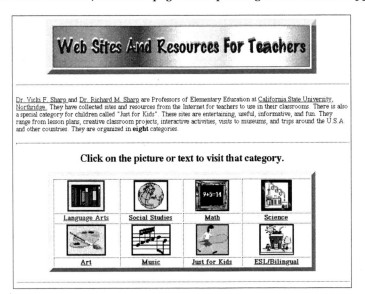

5. Wait until the page is fully loaded on your screen. You will see the word *Done* or the words *Document: Done* at the bottom of the screen.

6. You are now ready to explore *links*, or connections, to other Web pages. Links are words that are underlined or displayed in a different color, or are pictures that have a colored border around them. (In the descriptions of Web sites in this book, you are sometimes directed to navigate through specific links, which appear as capitalized words, e.g., Table of Contents.)

7. Click an underlined word link, shown in this illustration:

or a picture link, shown in this one:

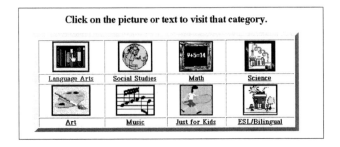

Note: When the mouse pointer passes over a live link, it becomes a hand.

Tips for Netscape Communicator and Internet Explorer Users

Other browsers work similarly to Netscape Communicator and Internet Explorer, so these tips are applicable for other browsers as well.

- When you type a URL in the Location or Open box, you can omit the http:// part of the URL; it will still work.

- Use the Back button to return to the previous site or page.

- If you cannot open a site with a given URL, use a search tool, such as Infoseek, Yahoo!, Ask Jeeves, Excite, Snap.com, About.com, Infind.com, Magellan, or AltaVista. In the search box, type the title of the site exactly as it appears (not its URL). The search tool might pick up the new URL for the title entered. The All-in-One Search Page (see Appendix 2) features a compilation of the various search tools you can use to help you find things on the Internet. The URL for the All-in-One Search Page is www.allonesearch.com/.

- When using a search engine you can narrow your search and avoid thousands of unnecessary hits. For example, when using Yahoo!, click the Options button and try using an "exact phrase" match. In Yahoo! you can also scroll to the bottom of the page and click other search engines that are listed.

- When searching, avoid generic or commonly used words. For example, a search for "baseball" might be too general and will deliver a tremendous number of matches. A search for "1970 World Series" is much better. The best searches will use terms, words, or phrases that correspond to words, terms, or phrases used in the documents you want to find.

- Most search engines let you link your search terms with words such as "and," "or," or "minus" (-), as well as search for phrases by placing the words in quotation marks. For example, you might search for "Stan Musial and World Series," which would give you information on both topics. If you replace "and" with "or," the search would be directed to identify one topic or the other. If you replace the "and" with the minus sign (no spaces), the engine will find the pages that contain references to Stan Musial but not the World Series. The connectors vary with the search engines. Check your search engine's help page for more tips.

- When you find a site you like, bookmark it so that you don't have to enter the URL for the site again.

  - From Netscape Communicator's **Bookmarks** menu, select **Add Bookmark**. The site will now be listed under the **Bookmarks** menu, and Netscape Communicator will take you to the site whenever you select it.

  - From Internet Explorer's **Favorites** menu, select **Add to Favorites**. Type the name for the site or use the name supplied. Click the OK button. The site will now be listed under the Favorites List, and Internet Explorer will take you to the site whenever you select it.

- The print size on a page may be too small for easy reading. However, most browsers let you change the size of the words as displayed on the screen.

  - In Netscape Communicator 4.5, from the **Edit** menu, choose **Preferences**. In the Preferences dialog box, from the Category scroll list, choose Fonts under Appearance. Choose a different size or type of font.

    *Note: Netscape 3.0 uses the menu path—**General Preferences-Fonts**.*

⏿ In Internet Explorer, go to the **View** menu, point to **Text Size**, and then choose a larger or smaller font for the text on that page.

⏿ If you just print the information from the site, you might get pages you do not need. To avoid this, go to Print Preview and determine how many pages you need. Now specify in the Print dialog box which pages you want to print. (If your browser does not have Print Preview, arbitrarily set a fixed number of pages in the Print dialog box.

⏿ Instead of printing pages, you can save them with the Save As feature in your browser. You have a choice of Source or Text. If you select Text, the pages will have no colors or formatting and can be opened with your word processor. If you select Source, the document is saved as an HTML document with color and formatting. The graphics must be saved separately.

⏿ In Netscape Communicator, press the mouse button while on a graphic. When the dialog box pops up, select "Save this image as."

⏿ In Internet Explorer, right-click the graphic. Then click Save Picture As on the short menu that appears.

Be sure to use the contact information on the Web page to request permission to use a graphic, and credit the source if you use it. Look for Web sites that give users permission to use the graphics for noncommercial purposes.

⏿ You can search long Web pages for a specific word or words.

⏿ In Netscape Communicator, press Command-F (⌘-F) on your keyboard. Type the word in the dialog box. Then click Find in the dialog box, or press Return on your keyboard. The word will appear highlighted.

⏿ In Internet Explorer, press Control + F (Ctrl + F) on your keyboard in the dialog box that appears, type the word, and then click Find Next. The word will appear highlighted.

Tips for Finding Inaccessible URLs

Be forewarned that Internet resources come and go with amazing speed. We cannot guarantee that all of the sites included in this book will be accessible when you try to open them. You might find messages such as: "404 Not Found" or "No DNS entry exists for this server." Here are some tips that might help you locate the site when you receive these types of messages.

⏿ Try opening the site again a few seconds later. Sometimes that works because the Internet computer serving the documents may be down temporarily or it may be so busy that you can't get in at the moment. Occasionally, the problem may be caused by your Internet Service Provider or commercial online service, which may be having problems with its Internet lines.

⏿ If you have waited more than 50 seconds and think that the site should have loaded by then, click the Stop button. Then click Reload.

⏿ Make sure you have spelled the URL exactly as it is printed in this book, using upper- and lowercase letters where appropriate. The Web is case sensitive, so "Csun" is not the same as "csun."

⏿ If suddenly your sites are not loading, you may have to go offline and reboot your system.

- ✺ To load a site faster, turn off the graphics and sound options on your browser. Although graphics and audio files are great, they take forever to load. In most instances, you can make text-only loading your browser's default setting. After seeing the site, you can turn on those options and return to examine the site again.

- ✺ If you can't find a site, you can sometimes physically modify your URL to get the page you desire. For example, when you try to dial up the Medical Matrix: Patient Education page at www.medmatrix.org/SPages/Patient_Education_and_ Support.stm, you may get an error message. Try deleting the final segment "Patient_Education_and_Support.stm" and press Return or Enter. Continue removing segments from the URL up to the forward slashes until it works. For this example, the URL www.medmatrix.org/ will work.

- ✺ Because the Web is always changing, sites switch servers, change their names, or just disappear forever. In many cases the old location will point you to the site's new location. If this is not the case, try using the company's name or product names in the URL. For instance, to find information about Apple Computing, type www.apple.com/. If this procedure doesn't work, go to a search engine and type Apple Computing.

- ✺ Many sites maintain numerous servers to accommodate high volume. To make sure the servers don't become overloaded, most Web masters limit the number of users. To overcome this difficulty, try another server. For example Netscape Communicator numbers its servers. If you can't access ftp://ftp3.netscape.com/, try ftp://ftp4.netscape.com/, and so forth.

- ✺ Finally, instead of looking through one search engine at a time, try using the search engine MetaCrawler, which allows you to search several engines at the same time. MetaCrawler can be found at www.metacrawler.com/. Another choice is Infind.com, which can be found at www.infind.com.

Note: The "Best Search Tools" is a guide that describes and compares information on all the major search engines. Its URL is: http://infopeople.org/src/schools.htm

Art

Art Projects

www.bway.net/~starlite/projects.htm

Art Projects, by Barbara Sonek, contains a collection of projects to do in K-12 classrooms.

The Art Room

www.arts.ufl.edu/art/rt_room/
@rtroom_home.html

The Art Room features a variety of classroom projects for Grades 3-12 in the Doorway section. This section also includes other useful art activities, including the Artifacts Center.

Art Takes Time

http://members.aol.com/TWard64340/
Index.htm

Art Takes Time, created by Tabitha Ward for elementary school students, contains a collection of lesson plans for various artistic movements from cave art to modern art.

ArtsEdNet

www.artsednet.getty.edu/

ArtsEdNet is an online arts education service for Grades K-12 sponsored by the Getty Center for Education in the Arts. The site includes online exhibits, the latest trends in art education, lesson plans, and other curriculum resources.

ArtsEdNet Lesson Plans

www.artsednet.getty.edu/ArtsEdNet/
Resources/index.html

ArtsEdNet Lesson Plans is an online service for K-12 arts education from the Getty Center for Education in the Arts. Teachers can find innovative lesson plans for the elementary school, middle school, and high school levels.

Crayola Art Education Lesson Plans

http://education.crayola.com/lessons/

Crayola Art Education Lesson Plans provide K-12 teachers with a variety of lesson plans that help guide students to recognize that creative communication involves not only language and visual arts, but social studies, science, and math. Users can search by products (crayons, markers, colored pencils, etc.), subject area, and age.

Explore Art

http://members.aol.com/powers8696/
artindex.html

Explore Art is authored by Connie M. Powers and provides lesson plans, activities, and links to additional sites for art fun and games.

Eyes on Art

www.kn.pacbell.com/wired/art/art.html

Eyes on Art, sponsored by Pacific Bell, provides seven visual art, Web-based lesson plans and a teacher's guide for K-12 classes.

Favorite Lessons

www.artswire.org/kenroar/lessons/lessons.html

Favorite Lessons features plans and activities for Grades K-12. Click a category to find a step-by-step explanation for a variety of topics, including Matisse Face Masterpiece, Table Murals, Monster Transformation, Masks and More Masks, and Too Loose Posters. The site also includes a form for submitting your favorite lesson.

KinderArt

www.kinderart.com/lessons.htm

KinderArt, provided by the Jarea Art Studio, features more than 100 free art lesson plans of every kind for kids ages 4-12. Topics include drawing, painting, printmaking, sculpture, multicultural art, cross-curricular art lessons, and coloring pages. The site also offers seasonal activities and art recipes in the Kinderart Littles section.

Modern Art Lesson Plans

www.utah.edu/umfa/modern.html

Modern Art Lesson Plans, for Grades 7-12, contains a collection of lesson plans from the Utah Museum of Fine Arts on the work of modern artists, such as Robert Indiana, Victor Vasarely, and Andy Warhol.

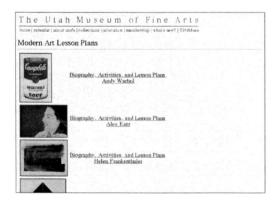

Visual Arts 8 to 10

www.bced.gov.bc.ca/irp/visart810/vatoc.htm

Visual Arts 8 to 10, provided by British Columbia's Ministry of Education, contains an integrated resource package of lesson plans for the visual arts in Grades 8, 9, and 10.

Visual Arts 11 and 12

www.bced.gov.bc.ca/irp/va1112/vatoc.htm

Visual Arts 11 and 12 provided by British Columbia's Ministry of Education, contains an integrated resource package of lesson plans for the visual arts in Grades 11 and 12.

A. Pintura: Art Detective

www.eduweb.com/pintura/

A. Pintura: Art Detective, produced by Educational Web Adventures, is an online game about art history and art composition suitable for Grades 4 and up. Students learn how to look at art by becoming "Art Detectives" and traveling to some of the world's major museums. As the detectives search for famous artworks, they complete exercises and learn about the artists and their art. A worksheet for assessment and accountability and a teacher key for guidance in correcting are available.

About.com: Art for Kids

http://artforkids.tqn.com/

About.com: Art for Kids provides a wide variety of art education sites for Grades K-12. The site includes online coloring books and printable coloring pages, as well as many activities and games.

Art Capades for K-3 Bilingual

www.kn.pacbell.com/wired/capades/

Art Capades for K-3 Bilingual, sponsored by Pacific Bell, features online activities for young bilingual children accompanied by tips for using the activities in the classroom.

Art Game

www.thru.com/art/game/

Art Game by ArtNet Italia allows kids test their ability to recognize art styles. The game is played in a number of turns in which different artworks are displayed in a central frame. The student's task is to select, in a limited time, one of the pictures in the side bars that has the same style as the central one, namely that was painted by the same artist.

Art Safari

http://artsafari.moma.org/

Art Safari allows kids to explore paintings and sculptures from the Museum of Modern Art accompanied by a series of questions in which they are encouraged to write about what they observe. They can also submit their own art work.

Art Teacher on the Net

www.artmuseums.com/

Art Teacher on the Net provides a list of annotated links to numerous art projects for Grades 4-12.

Coloring.com

http://coloring.com/

Coloring.com is an interactive coloring book for primary school pupils. Kids can color pictures online from a variety of categories and e-mail their pictures to family and friends.

Craft Finder

http://family.go.com/Categories/crafts/

Craft Finder, by *Family Fun Magazine*, is an interactive Web site offering elementary school kids the chance to select materials from a list that Craft Finder then puts together and suggests ideas for great projects.

Emmett Scott's Arts & Activities

www.cartooncorner.com/artspage.html

Emmett Scott's Arts & Activities, for Grades K–5, provides step-by-step instructions for drawing cartoons, as well as special tricks for creating them.

Joseph Wu's Origami Page

www.origami.vancouver.bc.ca/

Joseph Wu's Origami Page is the ultimate origami site, with extensive resources and information for K–12 teachers.

Kennedy Center's ArtsEdge

http://artsedge.kennedy-center.org/

Kennedy Center's ArtsEdge provides a forum where teachers and students can share information and ideas that support the arts in the K–12 curriculum.

M Education

www.metmuseum.org/htmlfile/education/
kid.html

M Education sponsored by the Metropolitan Museum of Art provides kids with online art games and Web activities. Also available are links to art programs and resources for families and students.

Stage Hand Puppets:
The Activity Page

www3.ns.sympatico.ca/onstage/puppets/

Stage Hand Puppets: The Activity Page, for elementary classes, contains tips and patterns for making paper and scrap hand puppets. The site also includes short puppet plays written by kids.

World Art Treasures
WWW Server

http://sgwww.epfl.ch/BERGER/index.html

World Art Treasures WWW Server, sponsored by the Jacques-Edouard Berger Foundation, presents a series of online art programs. These include art from Egypt, China, Japan, India, Myanmar/Burma, Laos, Cambodia, and Thailand. Other programs include the works of Sandro Botticelli and Johannes Vermeer.

Yahoo! Arts: Art History: Masters

www.yahoo.com/Arts/Artists/Masters/

Yahoo! Arts: Art History: Masters is a Yahoo! index with links to information on the lives and works of famous artists from around the world.

Asian Arts

www.webart.com/asianart/

Asian Arts is an electronic journal for the study and exhibition of the arts of Asia. For an online tour, click Exhibitions and Galleries. The site includes articles and links to other relevant resources.

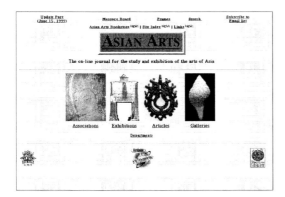

Diego Rivera

www.diegorivera.com/diego_home_eng.html

Diego Rivera is an exhibit that provides an in-depth study of the life and work of one of Mexico's most famous artists. A Spanish version is available.

Francisco Goya

http://goya.unizar.es/MainMenu_en.html

Francisco Goya presents the life of the famous Spanish artist accompanied by illustrations of his important works. A Spanish version is available.

Frida Kahlo Home Page

www.cascade.net/kahlo.html

Frida Kahlo Home Page presents the life and work of the famous Mexican artist.

The Global Show-n-Tell Museum

www.telenaut.com/gst/

The Global Show-n-Tell Museum provides a place where children of all ages can exhibit their art. There are detailed instructions on how kids can submit their work.

Museo del Prado

www.mcu.es/prado/index_eng.html

Museo del Prado offers information about the museum itself, a quick tour of 49 of its best-known works of art, a temporary exhibit celebrating the 250th anniversary of Goya, and links to other museums on the Web. A Spanish-language version is available.

Museums for Children

www.comlab.ox.ac.uk/oucl/users/
jonathan.bowen/children.html#museums

Museums for Children, maintained by Jonathan Bowen, presents links to children's museums throughout the world.

Treasures of The Louvre

www.paris.org/Musees/Louvre/Treasures/

Treasures of The Louvre presents Paintings; Egyptian Antiquities; Oriental Antiquities; Greek, Etruscan, and Roman Antiquities; Sculpture; Prints and Drawings; and Objets d'Art.

World Wide Web Virtual Library Museums Page

www.comlab.ox.ac.uk/archive/other/
museums.html

World Wide Web Virtual Library Museums Page contains museums by country and continent, as well as selected virtual museums.

Bilingual Education

Amigos

http://edweb.sdsu.edu/people/cguanipa/
amigos/

Amigos is an interactive online site for ethnically diverse middle school and high school students, parents, teachers, and interested adults. They can share stories, swap experiences, find information, or ask questions. Spanish and English versions are available.

Bilingual Books for Kids

www.bilingualbooks.com/

Bilingual Books for Kids provides a top-10 list and ordering information for books written with Spanish and English appearing side-by-side. The books introduce bilingual skills, increase language and learning abilities, and heighten awareness of many cultures.

Center for the Study of Books in Spanish for Children and Adolescents

www.csusm.edu/campus_centers/csb/

Center for the Study of Books in Spanish for Children and Adolescents is sponsored by California State University at San Marcos. The center endeavors to maintain strong ties with organizations interested in meeting the needs of young readers. The center provides a schedule of workshops, names and addresses of publishers, bibliographies, and listings of recommended books. A Spanish version of the Web site is available.

Cinco de Mayo

http://latino.sscnet.ucla.edu/demo/cinco.html

Cinco de Mayo is a pictorial tour of the famous battle that celebrates the victory of Mexican forces over the French in the 19th century.

Cuentos de Ika Bremer

www.ika.com/cuentos/

Cuentos de Ika Bremer features interactive online stories in Spanish. These "cuentos" help Spanish-speaking students enrolled in bilingual education programs enhance their first-language reading comprehension skills. English and German versions are also available.

Electronic Textbook: Bilingual Education

www.ecsu.ctstateu.edu/depts/edu/
textbooks/bilingual.html

Electronic Textbook: Bilingual Education provides links to various information on the Internet concerning bilingual education.

Enlaces bilingües para niños y maestros

http://members.tripod.com/~hamminkj/
bilingue.html

Internet sites, mostly in Spanish, for elementary school pupils. They include games, poems, and stories. In addition, there are links to lesson plans for teachers and information for parents.

Estrellita Accelerated Beginning Spanish Reading

www.estrellita.com/index.html

Estrellita Accelerated Beginning Spanish Reading provides a description of an educational reading program in Spanish for Spanish speakers. The program can be used by teachers in elementary school bilingual classrooms. Scroll down the page and click these links for additional information and materials for teaching in bilingual classrooms: Bilingual Education Resources on the Net, Primary Education (K–3) Resources For Bilingual Educators, and Latino Resources on the Net.

Fiesta de Muertos

http://mexico.udg.mx/Tradiciones/
Muertos/muertos.html

Fiesta de Muertos, written entirely in Spanish, is an online resource containing photos and information about this popular fiesta.

Fiesta de muertos

La Fiesta de Muertos se celebra en todo nuestro territorio de manera más o menos similar, aunque en cada región tiene sus peculiaridades.

Juegos y Canciones para Niños

www.hevanet.com/dshivers/juegos/

Spanish games and songs for children. Most of the songs included come from a CD called Naranja Dulce: Juegos Infantiles Compañia Infantil de Televicentro de Armando Torres. The CD is published by BMG in Mexico.

Kokone

www.kokone.com.mx/

This interactive online Spanish-language kids' site is about Mexico's culture. El Tlacuache, an opossum-like creature, is the animated guide. Students will find games and riddles, a Latin American cooking section, an animals and eco-adventure section, a life through the eyes of the children of Mexico section, a literature section, and a historical section.

Lugares en Español para Niños

www.ala.org/parentspage/greatsites/
arts2.html#g

Los sitios se recomiendan para los niños de edad pre-escolar hasta, e incluyendo, los catorce años, sus padres y aquellos quienes los cuidan.

Mundo Latino Rinconcito

www.mundolatino.org/rinconcito/

An interactive site that features activities, games, and stories for Spanish-speaking elementary school pupils. Mundo Latino Rinconcito also includes a bulletin board for children and links to more children's sites.

National Clearinghouse for Bilingual Education

www.ncbe.gwu.edu/

National Clearinghouse for Bilingual Education (NCBE) is funded by the U.S. Department of Education's Office of Bilingual Education and Minority Languages Affairs (OBEMLA). NCBE collects, analyzes, and disseminates information related to the effective education of linguistically and culturally diverse K–12 learners in the United States. The site includes an online library, language and education links, databases, and links to publishers and distributors of teaching materials. You can also subscribe to an e-mail news bulletin and an electronic discussion group.

Paso Partners

www.sedl.org/scimath/pasopartners/
pphome.html

Paso Partners provides bilingual (English/Spanish)
lesson plans for K–3 students that integrate
science, math, and language. Plans include Five
Senses (Los Cinco Sentidos), Spiders, (Las Arañas),
and Dinosaurs (Los Dinosauros).

Paso Partners - Integrating Mathematics, Science and Language

A Bilingual Instructional Program

Introduction

Integrating Mathematics, Science and Language: An Instructional Program is a two-volume bilingual curriculum and resources guide developed by Paso Partners - a partnership of three public schools, an institution of higher education, and SEDL specialists. The resource is designed to help elementary school teachers organize their classrooms and instructional activities in order to increase achievement of Hispanic primary-grade children whose first language is not English. The guide offers a curriculum plan, instructional strategies and activities, suggested teacher and student materials, and assessment procedures.

Spanish language translation: Accompanying each complete unit in English is a Spanish version of background information for the teacher, as well as a Spanish version of the formal introductory portion of the lesson cycle.

Hypertext Markup Language (HTML) versions

Volume 1: (Grade K)

Drama

Drama 8 to 10

www.bced.gov.bc.ca/irp/drama810/drtoc.htm

Drama 8 to 10, from British Columbia's Ministry of Education, features an integrated resource package of lesson plans for teaching dance and drama in Grades 8, 9, and 10.

The Drama Teacher's Resource Room

www3.sk.sympatico.ca/erachi/

The Drama Teacher's Resource Room features creative and challenging experiences for students in the drama classroom. It offers lesson plans; articles on costume, props, set design, lighting, and scenic painting; and links to other resources.

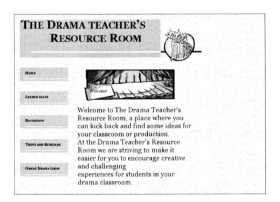

The Lesson Plan Exchange for Teachers of Theater

http://artemis.austinc.edu/acad/educ/ATPWeb/lesson.HTM

The Lesson Plan Exchange for Teachers of Theater is designed as a resource for secondary school theater teachers. Included are lesson plans for beginning theater, advanced theater, technical theater, production, and directing. The site also contains links to professional organizations, high school theater Web sites, and other theater-related sites.

Storytelling, Drama, Creative Dramatics, Puppetry & Readers Theater for Children & Young Adults

http://falcon.jmu.edu/~ramseyil/drama.htm

Storytelling, Drama, Creative Dramatics, Puppetry & Readers Theater for Children & Young Adults provides teachers with resources for oral interpretation of literature through dramatic activity, storytelling, and reader's theater. Among the links available are Reader's Theater Scripts and Lesson Plans K–8, which feature lessons on creative dramatics, creative thinking, creativity, elements in drama, exposition, script starters, and expressive speech.

British Theatre

http://britishtheatre.miningco.com/

British Theatre is the Mining Company's guide to the whole spectrum of British theater, from musicals to Shakespeare. The site looks at the performers and the writers, the stars and the wannabes. The site is suitable for high school English and drama classes.

Children's Creative Theatre

http://tqjunior.advanced.org/5291/

Children's Creative Theatre was produced by kids for kids. It features a short history of theater, a glossary of theater terms, creative dramatics games and activities, a skit, quizzes, and more. The teacher's resource section contains cross-curriculum based ideas and is organized by grade level and subject area.

Children's Theatre

http://faculty-web.at.nwu.edu/theater/tya/

Children's Theatre features information and resources.

Dramatists Play Service

www.dramatists.com/text/main.html

Dramatists Play Service has worked with both nonprofessional and professional theater groups to provide plays available for production. Teachers will find a listing of plays by title, author, and number of characters, as well as information on obtaining nonprofessional performance rights.

The Educational Theatre Association

www.etassoc.org/eta-home.htm

The Educational Theatre Association (ETA) is devoted to promoting and supporting educational theater programs, primarily at the middle school and high school levels. ETA publishes a monthly magazine, *Dramatics*, and a quarterly publication, *Teaching Theatre*. For a list of useful and interesting theater-oriented sites on the World Wide Web, click The Resource Pool and then Education Links.

High School Theatre

www.fn.net/~east22/HSprograms.html

High School Theatre is maintained by the Theatre Arts Department at Wichita High School East. The site provides links to Acting; Broadway and Ticket Information; General Theatre; Magazines and Journals; Playwrights, Lyricists, and Composers; Publishers; and Technical Theatre. It also allows teachers and students to search a collection of other high school theater sites on the Web.

Playbill Online

www1.playbill.com/playbill/

Playbill Online provides theater listings, newsletters, a multimedia center, job opportunities, links to theater resources, and much more. This resource should interest anyone considering drama as a career.

Samuel French

www.samuelfrench.com/

Samuel French is the world's oldest play publisher and caters to film and theater professionals and students. It provides the largest selection of plays in the world. Teachers can browse an Alphabetical List of Book Titles.

The School Show Page

www.schoolshows.demon.co.uk/

The School Show Page contains a variety of online resources for school and youth theater in Grades K–12. You'll find articles on playwriting in the archive section, a list of plays and guides for the classroom in the download section, and new plays in the What's New section. You can also contact U.S. schools about their theater arts programs.

Scott's Theatre Links

www.theatre-link.com/

Scott's Theatre Links provides links to information about Broadway and Off-Broadway shows and their lyrics and music, as well as links to Shakespeare's works and Shakespeare festivals.

Theatre Central

www1.playbill.com/cgi-bin/plb/
central?cmd=start

Theatre Central provides a large directory of theater resources on the Web.

University High School Thespians Home Page

www.ilstu.edu/depts/labschl/uhigh/
depts/theatre/

University High School Thespians Home Page is affiliated with Illinois State University at Normal, Illinois, and provides high school drama students and teachers with links to information on playwrights and composers, theater magazines and journals, live theater and ticket information, auditions, and technical resources.

Yahoo! Arts: Drama: Musicals

www.yahoo.com/Arts/Performing_Arts/
Theater/Musicals/

Yahoo! Arts: Drama: Musicals provides relevant information for high school drama students and teachers. It includes links to Movies, Shows, Songwriters, and Theater Groups.

ESL

Adult Education ESL Teachers Guide

http://humanities.byu.edu/elc/Teacher/
TeacherGuideMain

Adult Education ESL Teachers Guide is written
and produced by C. Ray Graham and Mark M.
Walsh. The lesson plans can be adapted for
secondary school students. Links include
Beginning ESL Lessons and Accompanying Teacher
Training Modules, Intermediate ESL Lessons and
Accompanying Teacher Training Modules, and
Teaching Non-Literate Adults. All materials and
worksheets are provided.

English Club Teachers' Room

www.englishclub.net/teachers/index.htm

English Club Teachers' Room includes lesson
plans, activities, and handouts for teaching EFL
and ESL.

ESL Teacher Connection

www-personal.si.umich.edu/~jarmour/etc/
etchome.html

ESL Teacher Connection provides an open forum
in which ESL teachers can share their own
successful class activities and lesson plans with
other teachers. You can print, revise, and use the
lesson plans and activities found here.

The Internet TESL Journal for Teachers of ESL

www.aitech.ac.jp/~iteslj/

The Internet TESL Journal for Teachers of ESL is
a monthly Web magazine featuring lesson plans
and lesson ideas.

Karin's ESL Party Land

www.eslpartyland.com/

Karin's ESL Party Land provides teachers with
lesson plans and printable materials to use in
class and provides students with more than 50
interactive quizzes, 15 discussion forums, and
additional links.

PIZZAZ! A Resource for Scribblers and Teachers of English as a Second Language

http://darkwing.uoregon.edu/~leslieob/
pizzaz.html

**PIZZAZ! A Resource for Scribblers and Teachers
of English as a Second Language**, produced by
Leslie Opp-Beckman, is dedicated to providing
creative writing activities and reproducible
handouts for use in ESL classrooms for
Grades 7–12.

Dave's ESL Cafe on the Web

www.pacificnet.net/~sperling/eslcafe.html

Dave's ESL Cafe on the Web is open 24 hours a day for ESL students and teachers from around the world. Scroll down the page and select from a variety of cafe items. You can take an interactive quiz in the ESL Quiz Center, receive help with questions related to English in the ESL Help Center, search for something in the cafe or on the Web at the One-Stop ESL Search Page, share your experiences with others on the ESL Idea Page, read and add your own writings to the ESL Graffiti Wall, or ask a question of Dave on the ESL Question Page. There are also links to other ESL information for both students and teachers, an interactive message exchange, an ESL e-mail connection, and a job center. The site is suitable for Grades 9-12.

English Grammar Links for ESL Students

www.gl.umbc.edu/~kpokoy1/grammar1.htm

English Grammar Links for ESL Students, created by Karen M. Hartman, provides links to grammar references, exercises, and quizzes that can help ESL teachers and students in Grades 7-12.

ESL Standards for Pre-K-12 Students

www.tesol.edu/assoc/k12standards/it/01.html

ESL Standards for Pre-K-12 Students is clustered by grade level (pre-K-3, 4-8, and 9-12) and addresses varying degrees of proficiency (beginner, intermediate, advanced), as well as the needs of ESL students with limited formal schooling. The standards use vignettes of actual instructional sequences in which teachers help students meet the standards in diverse settings (e.g., social studies, math).

everythingESL.Net

www.everythingESL.net/

everythingESL.Net features resources for ESL teachers working with K-12 language minority students. The site includes lesson plans, information, staff inservicing, activities, bulletin boards, and more.

Learning English on the Web

www.lang.uiuc.edu/r-li5/esl/

Learning English on the Web is a starting point for ESL learners in Grades 7-12 who want to learn English on the World Wide Web. The site includes listening, speaking, reading, and writing activities.

Taiwan Teacher

www.geocities.com/Athens/Delphi/1979/games.html#index

The **Taiwan Teacher** provides games, ideas, and activities for ESL/EFL teachers. Although the games are meant for children, many can be adapted for all levels of English language learners.

TESL: Lessons

www.aitech.ac.jp/~iteslj/links/TESL/Lessons/

TESL: Lessons is sponsored by the *Internet TESL Journal* and features links to a large variety of lesson plans and activities relevant for teachers of Grades 7-12.

TESOL Online

www.tesol.edu/

TESOL Online, from Teachers of English to Speakers of Other Languages, the international professional association of ESL teachers, includes links to publications available from TESOL, as well as selected articles from *TESOL Journal* and *TESOL Quarterly*.

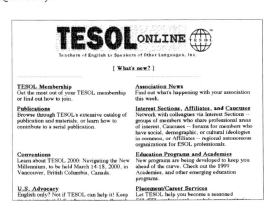

Foreign Language

Arts and Foreign Language Instructional Resources

http://artsedge.kennedy-center.org/cs/forlang.html

Arts and Foreign Language Instructional Resources, developed by ARTSEDGE, provides lesson plans and online activities for foreign language students at the middle and high school levels. The plans make use of art, cooking, music, puppets, and literature.

Blue Web'n Learning Applications

www.kn.pacbell.com/wired/bluewebn/

Blue Web'n Learning Applications, provided by Pacific Bell, includes lessons, activities, projects, resources, references, and tools. Scroll to Content Table, Foreign Language to find the materials.

Cooperative Learning in Modern Languages

www.geocities.com/Paris/LeftBank/3852/cooplearn.html

Cooperative Learning in Modern Languages was prepared by Pete Jones of the Pine Ridge Secondary School in Ontario (Canada). The site features lessons useful for creating a student-centered language class, which teachers can print out. Several of the activities are available for languages other than French.

Creative French Teaching Methods

www3.sympatico.ca/heather.zaitlin/TEACHER.HTM

Creative French Teaching Methods is designed specifically for the French teacher and provides links to lesson plans, teacher resource pages, and curriculum planning ideas, as well as to popular songs and activities for watching international TV.

Especially Español

http://edweb.sdsu.edu/edfirst/spanish/

Especially Español contains lesson plans and online activities for elementary, middle, and high school levels. Additional resources are also included.

Foreign Language Resources on the Internet Illinois State University

http://mdavies.for.ilstu.edu/class/

Foreign Language Resources on the Internet presents links to nearly 600 minilesson plans based on Web sites dealing with a number of foreign language topics. The lesson plans were created by participants from Illinois State University.

Foreign Language Units

http://commtechlab.msu.edu/sites/letsnet/NoFrames/Subjects/fl/index.html

Foreign Language Units was developed by a collaborative team at Michigan State University and provides elementary, middle, and high school teachers and students with online instructional units. Each lesson plan within the unit contains: a brief description, objectives, materials and resources, activity description, and Internet resources.

Hot Internet Sites in Español

www.kn.pacbell.com/wired/fil/pages/listspanish.html

Hot Internet Sites in Español is an Internet hotlist of Spanish resources created by Beth Bustamante, Pacific Bell Education First, and appropriate for Grades K-12. Teachers will find resources for students who are native speakers as well as for students learning Spanish as a foreign language. Included are lesson plans and activities for use with or without a computer.

Internet Activities for Foreign Language Classes

http://members.aol.com/maestro12/web/wadir.html

Internet Activities for Foreign Language Classes contains online lesson plans and student worksheets for using foreign language Web sites in high school German, French, Japanese, and Spanish classes. Each worksheet presents students with questions, activities, and corresponding Web sites students must access to complete the assignment. Worksheets can be printed out and used by the whole class or by individuals for homework.

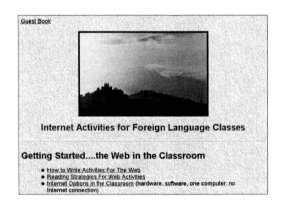

Lesson Ideas Para La Clase

www.teachspanish.com/lessons.html

Lesson Ideas Para La Clase, from TeachSpanish.Com, shares Spanish and ESL lesson plans and activities contributed by classroom teachers.

Advanced Placement Program

www.collegeboard.org/ap/indx002.html

Advanced Placement Program, provided by the College Board Online, features tips for teachers and students, information about AP classes and exams, and related Web sites for all AP subjects, including French, German, and Spanish.

AltaVista Translation Service

http://babelfish.altavista.digital.com/ cgi-bin/translate?

AltaVista Translation Service allows users to enter text or a URL and have it translated into another language.

American Association of Teachers of French

http://aatf.utsa.edu/

American Association of Teachers of French (AATF) promotes the study of French through its 75 chapters and its two official publications: *French Review* and *National Bulletin*. The What's New at AATF selection on the AATF site includes links to other sites of interest to teachers of French.

American Classical League

www.umich.edu/~acleague/

American Classical League (ACL) provides its membership and other interested people with resources of importance to the teaching and study of the Classics. The ACL Web site lets you select Secondary School Programs in Classics for the e-mail addresses and Web pages of secondary school programs. You can also select Undergraduate Programs in Classics, where information about undergraduate course offerings may be found. There are additional links to Teaching Tools, Professional Resources, Journals and Publications, and Classics, as well as education-related links.

American Council on the Teaching of Foreign Languages

www.actfl.org/index.htm

American Council on the Teaching of Foreign Languages (ACTFL) is the professional association that represents teachers of all languages at all educational levels. The ACTFL site contains information on a variety of topics, including professional development programs, national standards in foreign language education, publications, special interest groups, and related organizations.

ClicNet

www.swarthmore.edu/Humanities/clicnet/

ClicNet édite ou localise des ressources virtuelles en français pour les étudiants, les enseignants de français langue étrangère (FLE) ou langue seconde (FLS), et tous ceux qui s'intéressent aux cultures, aux arts et aux littératures francophones. No English version is available.

Clip Art Collection for Foreign/Second Language Instruction

www.sla.purdue.edu/fll/JapanProj/FLClipart/

Clip Art Collection for Foreign/Second Language Instruction provides a series of hand-drawn pictures illustrating verbs, adjectives, and common nouns that teachers can print out and use in the classroom.

Communication Connections

www.widomaker.com/~ldprice/#Pelusa

Communication Connections, designed by Lora Price, a teacher at Gloucester High School in Virginia, is a menu of Web sites dedicated to the study, use, and enjoyment of languages. Although many cultures and languages are represented, specialized listings have been provided for French, German, Latin, Italian, Japanese, and Spanish. At this site, you can consult original sources, use a foreign language dictionary, take a language course, navigate metro systems, read the daily news, or listen to music from the country of your choice.

Fast and Friendly French for Fun

http://hyperion.advanced.org/12447/

Fast and Friendly French for Fun is an online interactive site geared for the middle school level. There's a guided tour of the site; a Geography, People, and Food tour of France; a set of introductory lessons, including All-Purpose Phrases; and a game.

Foreign Language News and Magazine Page

http://libraries.mit.edu/humanities/flnews/

Foreign Language News and Magazine Page features online newspapers and magazines in a variety of languages including Chinese, French, German, Italian, Japanese, Portuguese, Russian, and Spanish.

Foreign Language Study Abroad for Teachers

www.csun.edu/~hcedu013/
LanguageAbroad.html

Foreign Language Study Abroad for Teachers features links to hundreds of foreign language schools in dozens of countries where teachers can upgrade their language skills. Also included is a directory of High School Foreign Exchange and Language Study Programs suitable for teenagers.

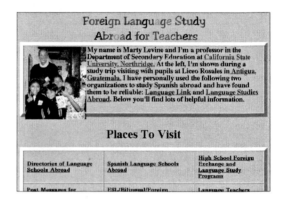

Foreign Language Teaching Forum

www.cortland.edu/www_root/flteach/
flteach.html#resources

Foreign Language Teaching Forum (FL Teach) provides resources for classroom activities, curriculum, and syllabus design. It features Web links to foreign language resources organized by language. Information is provided on subscribing to a mailing list that allows you to ask a question about a topic, share an idea or lesson plan, or just read what your fellow teachers say. Messages will appear in your e-mail. You can also search the FL Teach archives and read previous messages.

German Studies Trails on the Web

www2.uncg.edu/~lixlpurc/german.html

German Studies Trails on the Web, compiled by Andreas Lixl-Purcell, professor of German at the University of North Carolina at Greensboro, lists some of the most useful interdisciplinary German resources on the World Wide Web. You can select from a variety of topics, such as German Language and Culture (Sprache und Landeskunde), Arts and Humanities (Kunst und Wissenschaft), and Education and Research (Unterricht und Forschung).

High School Foreign Exchange and Language Study Programs

www.csun.edu/~hcedu013/karin.html

High School Foreign Exchange and Language Study Programs was designed by Karin Levine, a Spanish teacher at Thousand Oaks (California) High School. The site features links to organizations sponsoring high school foreign exchange programs and language study programs abroad for teens.

Intercultural E-Mail Classroom Connections

www.stolaf.edu/network/iecc/

The **Intercultural E-Mail Classroom Connections (IECC)** mailing lists are provided by St. Olaf College as a free service to help teachers and classes link with partners in other countries and cultures for e-mail classroom pen pal and project exchanges.

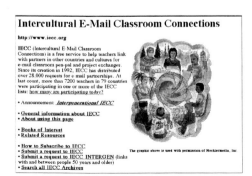

Language Quest Software

www.languagequest.com/

Language Quest Software features language software, specialized word processors, translators, programs for kids, and fonts for all languages of the world. The site provides an online catalog.

Language Resources and Technology Information

www.cet.middlebury.edu/herren/pages/langTech.html

Language Resources and Technology Information provides resources for foreign language teachers and students interested in computer-assisted and technology-enhanced language learning. Also included in the site is information on foreign language software available on the Internet, online foreign language newspapers, and foreign language courses on the Web.

The Latin Page (Salvete Ad Paginam Latinam)

www.geocities.com/Athens/Acropolis/3773/

The Latin Page (Salvete Ad Paginam Latinam) provides general classroom resources designed primarily for the Latin teacher in Grades 7–12. Some projects may be adapted for the lower grades.

Latinteach Classroom Ideas and Projects

www.geocities.com/Athens/Styx/1790/ideas.html

Latinteach Classroom Ideas and Projects features some of the best ideas and projects from the Latinteach Mailing List for teachers of Latin at all levels.

Les Misérables—The Complete Multilingual Libretto

www.arts.uci.edu/kelson/les-mis/

Les Misérables—The Complete Multilingual Libretto, designed and maintained by Kelson Vibber, features French, German, and English lyrics for the entire musical.

Resources for Students and Teachers of French as a Second Language

www.uottawa.ca/~weinberg/french.html

Resources for Students and Teachers of French as a Second Language is provided by the University of Ottawa, Canada. It features exercises and resources for students; resources for teachers; French in Canada, outside Quebec, in Quebec, and in France; Francophonie in the world; news and discussion groups; and miscellaneous links.

Tecla

www.bbk.ac.uk/Departments/Spanish/ TeclaHome.html

Tecla, an electronic magazine for learners and teachers of Spanish, is written by members of the Spanish Department at Birkbeck College, University of London. It appears weekly on the Web during the school year and consists of short readings followed by comprehension exercises.

Tennessee Bob's Famous French Links

www.utm.edu/departments/french/french.html

Tennessee Bob's Famous French Links provides useful resources for teachers and learners of French. Topics include Art and Special Image Exhibits; Literature and Music; Newspapers, Magazines, and Newsgroups; and Audiovisual (radio/TV).

Health Education/ Physical Education

California Physical Education Instruction

www.stan-co.k12.ca.us/calpe/Instruction.html

California Physical Education Instruction provides teachers with model lessons. Scroll to the bottom of the page to find sample lesson plans for the elementary, middle, and high school levels.

Health Lesson Ideas

http://pe.central.vt.edu/lessonideas/health/healthlp.html

Health Lesson Ideas, from PE Central (sponsored by Virginia Tech), provides lessons for elementary school, middle school, and high school students.

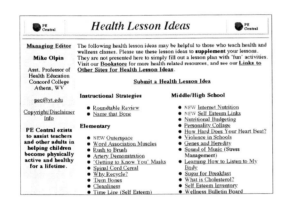

PE Central

http://pe.central.vt.edu/

PE Central is specifically designed for physical education teachers, students, interested parents, and adults. Sponsored by Virginia Tech, its goal is to provide the latest information about contemporary physical education programs for children and youth. The site includes assessment ideas, lesson plans, activities of the week, P.E. people on the Web, links to other relevant sites, and information on how to subscribe to a mailing list.

PE Lesson Ideas

http://pe.central.vt.edu/lessonideas/pelessonplans.html

PE Lesson Ideas, from PE Central (sponsored by Virginia Tech), provides useful lessons for pre-K, elementary school, middle school, and high school students.

PE Lesson Plans and Activities

www.ping.be/sportsmedia/Lesson.htm

PE Lesson Plans and Activities, from Sports Media, provides more than 50 lesson plans for all areas of the P.E. program.

Physical Education K to 7

www.bced.gov.bc.ca/irp/pek7/petoc.htm

Physical Education K to 7, produced by the British Columbia Ministry of Education, contains P.E. lesson plans for students at the K–7 level.

Physical Education 8 to 10

www.bced.gov.bc.ca/irp/pe810/petoc.htm

Physical Education 8 to 10, sponsored by the British Columbia Ministry of Education, features P.E. lesson plans for students in Grades 8–10.

Physical Education 11 and 12

www.bced.gov.bc.ca/irp/pe11_12/petoc.htm

Physical Education 11 and 12, from the British Columbia Ministry of Education, provides lesson plans for high school students.

Physical Education Lesson Plans

http://members.tripod.com/~pazz/lesson.html

Physical Education Lesson Plans is a place for physical educators to share lesson plans. New lessons are submitted often.

Adolescence Directory On-Line

http://education.indiana.edu/cas/adol/adol.html

Adolescence Directory On-Line (ADOL) is an electronic guide to information regarding adolescent issues and secondary education. It is maintained by the Center for Adolescent Studies, located in the School of Education, Indiana University, Bloomington. The site features electronic links to relevant health resources for teachers, kids, counselors, and parents. Link topics include Mental Health Issues, Health Issues, Conflict and Violence, Counselor Resources, and Teens Only.

Benny Goodsport

www.bennygoodsport.com/

Benny Goodsport provides information, activities, games, puzzles, and stories about sports and recreational activities for elementary school kids.

Dole 5 A Day Homepage

www.dole5aday.com/

Dole 5 A Day Homepage provides nutrition information about fruits and vegetables for elementary school students. It offers fun school activities for kids, and teachers can order a free CD-ROM from Dole.

Dr. Pribut's Running Injuries Page

www.clark.net/pub/pribut/spsport.html

Dr. Pribut's Running Injuries Page offers runners, coaches, and teachers information on running injuries and how to prevent them. It also includes links to other sports pages.

Fronske Health Center's Health Education Page

www.nau.edu/~fronske/he.html

Fronske Health Center's Health Education Page provides information relevant to high school health teachers. Click Health Brochure for links to topics ranging from alcohol and AIDS to fitness and infectious diseases.

Healthwise

www.columbia.edu/cu/healthwise/

Healthwise features *Go Ask Alice!* an interactive, health-related question-and-answer service on the Web. Health professionals at Columbia University provide the answers. Users can search archives for answers to previously asked questions.

International Food Information Council

http://ificinfo.health.org/

International Food Information Council (IFIC) offers a Web site that contains information about healthy and safe food choices for K–12 students. Click Information for Educators to find information about the new food label educational curriculum for Grades 10–12, food insight reprints, and videotapes.

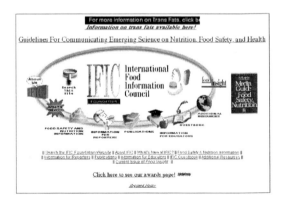

KidsHealth.Org

http://kidshealth.org/index2.html

KidsHealth.Org, a project sponsored by the Nemours Foundation Center for Biomedical Communication, is an interactive Web site providing health information. Click Parents, Teens or Kids to find relevant resources. Students can play games, participate in polls and quizzes, and read a health tip of the day. They can even enter one of their own health tips and win a T-shirt.

KidSource OnLine Healthcare

www.kidsource.com/kidsource/pages/
Health.html

KidSource OnLine Healthcare provides health care information for K–12 teachers and parents.

Multimedia Tutorials
for Children and Parents

http://galen.med.virginia.edu/~smb4v/
tutorial.html

Multimedia Tutorials for Children and Parents, sponsored by Children's Medical Center of the University of Virginia, provides tutorials on asthma, cerebral palsy, and gastroesophageal reflux, with additional topics coming soon. Each tutorial features text, graphics, sound, and video.

Resources for School
Health Educators

www.indiana.edu/~aphs/hlthk-12.html

Resources for School Health Educators, from the Department of Applied Health Science at Indiana University, provides teachers and high school students with a wide variety of relevant resources. Among its many links are those to information on school health education; national health organizations; alcohol, tobacco, and other drug education; violence prevention; first aid; sex education; and health education centers and museums.

SPARK Physical Education:
"P.E. for the 21st Century"

www.foundation.sdsu.edu/projects/spark/
index.html

SPARK Physical Education: "P.E. for the 21st Century" is an innovative K–6 physical education curriculum and staff development program. The SPARK program offers materials and services to schools and health organizations on a nonprofit basis through San Diego State University.

Sports Media

www.ping.be/~ping7330/

Sports Media is a nonprofit organization of physical education experts. The organization uses its Web site to present sports and physical education links and lesson plans. Original material and online advice is collected from coaches, educators, and other experts in all types of sports.

Worldguide Health & Fitness Forum

www.worldguide.com/hf.html

Worldguide Health & Fitness Forum provides high school physical education teachers, coaches, trainers, and athletes with links to a human anatomy lesson, exercise recommendations for power and speed, ideas on how to maintain a healthy heart, and nutritional information.

Yahoo! Recreation: Sports

www.yahoo.com/Recreation/Sports/

Yahoo! Recreation: Sports provides teachers, coaches, and kids with links to relevant information for all sports, from air hockey and wrestling to archery and water polo. The site also includes a link to Scoreboard, which provides up-to-the-minute scores and information. A search tool allows you to find more information about sports in the Yahoo! database.

Journalism

For Journalism Teachers Only

www.geocities.com/Athens/Aegean/6763

For Journalism Teachers Only contains a wealth of information and links for journalism teachers, publications advisers, and student editors.

The Freedom Forum: High School and College

www.freedomforum.org/FreedomForum/
resources/hs_and_coll/

The Freedom Forum: High School and College provides links to sites of interest to all who value freedom of the press. Links include Youth Guide to the First Amendment, Talking About Freedom, and High School Journalism.

Highwired.Net

www.highwired.net/

Highwired.Net is the world's largest network of online high schools. Using their FREE and easy-to-use Web publishing tools, teachers and students can create Internet sites to build their own high school paper online.

Indiana University High School Journalism Institute

www.journalism.indiana.edu/workshops/
HSJI/index.html

Indiana University High School Journalism Institute serves as a continuing education outreach program for secondary school students and their teachers. The institute provides summer workshops and a number of newsletters and other publications supportive of secondary school journalism education.

Journalism Education Association

www.spub.ksu.edu/~jea/

Journalism Education Association (JEA) has among its 1,600 members journalism teachers and publications advisers, media professionals, press associations, advisers' organizations, libraries, yearbook companies, newspapers, radio stations, and journalism departments. The site includes a menu with links to information about conferences, curriculum helps, scholarships, books, student press rights, newspapers on the Web, and job opportunities.

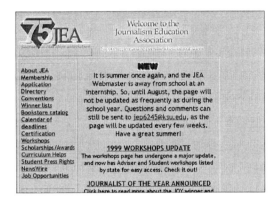

Journalism Education Association of Northern California

www.dcn.davis.ca.us/~jeanc/home.html

Journalism Education Association of Northern California (jeanc) provides excellent resources for high school journalism students and their advisers, including a copy of California's Education Code explaining students' free speech rights and responsibilities and a Model Publications Code. Information about the Student Press Law Center, the Freedom Forum, and the national Journalism Education Association's position on student press rights is given. The site also includes a list of other journalism sites on the Web.

KidNews

www.kidnews.com/

KidNews is a news and writing service for elementary school and middle school students and teachers around the world. Using this free exchange service, teachers and kids can gather news stories and ideas for their own school papers. KidNews includes news stories, feature stories, profiles, and sports stories, as well as information on other newspaper-related topics.

National Scholastic Press Association

http://studentpress.journ.umn.edu/

National Scholastic Press Association is a nonprofit membership organization serving student journalists and advisers. Information is available about summer journalism workshops, journalism competitions, e-mail discussion lists, *The Best of High School Press Online*, and links to hundreds of useful resources.

The Write Site to Explore the World of Journalism

www.writesite.org/

The Write Site to Explore the World of Journalism is an interactive journalism project for middle schools. The site features a Newsroom for Students, and an Editor's Desk for Teachers. By taking the monthly Classroom Challenge, students can see how their class stacks up against other Write Site schools.

Yahoo!'s Index of Newspapers K–12

www.yahoo.com/News/Newspapers/K_12/

Yahoo!'s Index of Newspapers K–12 features links to student-produced online newspapers that teachers and kids can use as a guide to improving their own school's publications.

Language Arts

A to Z Teacher Stuff: Children's Literature Activities Index

www.atozteacherstuff.com/stuff/literatu.html

A to Z Teacher Stuff provides more than 500 lesson plans and activities arranged alphabetically by book title for teaching children's literature in the elementary school. The site also includes many other language arts activities in the Thematic Units Index and in the teacher-submitted lesson plans section.

Academy Curricular Exchange

http://ofcn.org/cyber.serv/academy/ace/

The Academy Curricular Exchange offers lesson plans covering various subject areas for Grades K-12. To find more than 90 plans for language arts, click these links: Elementary School, Intermediate School, or High School.

ACCESS INDIANA Teaching & Learning Center

http://tlc.ai.org/

The ACCESS INDIANA Teaching & Learning Center provides a collection of language arts lesson plans for Grades K-12. To find them, click Teacher Lesson Plans in the Language Arts section.

Activity Search

www.eduplace.com/search/activity2.html

Activity Search, from Houghton Mifflin, features a curriculum database where K-8 teachers can search for language arts lesson plans/activities and other subject areas by grade level. Activities can also be browsed by theme.

ALI Units of Practice

http://ali.apple.com/

The Apple Learning Interchange (ALI) contains lessons (units of practice) created by teachers for integrating technology into the teaching and learning process for Grades K-12. Click Units and use the "subject" and "level" pull-down menus to find language arts lessons for English or literature. You can search the Resources section also to find language arts lesson plans as well as participate in an ongoing collaborative project sponsored by Apple.

Apply Learning Network: Technical and Professional Communications 12

http://cfaa.bridges.com/english.htm

The Apply Learning Network provides a collection of high school English lessons that connect classroom learning with real-life, workplace situations.

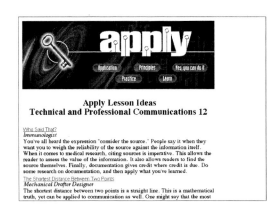

AskERIC Lesson Plans: Language Arts

http://ericir.syr.edu/Virtual/Lessons/Lang_arts/

AskERIC Lesson Plans: Language Arts provides a collection of nearly 100 language arts lesson plans contributed by teachers for Grades K-12. Links include Literature, Writing Composition, Reading, and Spelling. Each lesson plan features an overview, purpose, objectives, activities, and resource materials.

The Awesome Library: Language Arts Lesson Plans

www.neat-schoolhouse.org/Library/ Materials_Search/Lesson_Plans/ Language_Arts.html

The Awesome Library: Language Arts Lesson Plans contains a collection of hundreds of language arts lesson plans for Grades K-12.

Books@Random: Teacher Services

www.randomhouse.com/teachers.html

Random House provides a collection of Teacher's Guides for each of its separate divisions. Each guide contains background story information, discussion questions, comprehension questions, and, for Grades 6-12, related research topics. You can find a Teacher's Guide at Teachers@Random for Grades K-8, BDD Teacher's Resource Center for K-12, Jr.-Sr. High Teachers, and Random House Academic Marketing for Grades 9-12.

Big Sky Gopher Menu

gopher://bvsd.k12.co.us:70/11/ Educational_Resources/Lesson_Plans/ Big%20Sky/language_arts

Big Sky Gopher Menu features a collection of language arts lesson plans for Grades K-12, including reading and composition plans.

CanTeach

http://persweb.direct.ca/ikhan/

CanTeach, maintained by Iram Khan & James Hörner, provides a wide variety of elementary resources. In this section, teachers will find English language arts lesson plans as well as ready-to-use songs and poems for use on special days and events.

Carol Hurst's Children's Literature Site

www.carolhurst.com/titles/featuredtitles.html

Carol Hurst's Children's Literature Site contains a collection of lessons and activities to accompany more than 25 children's books in the Featured Books section. For a table of contents for the site, scroll to Getting Around Our Site and click Expanded Table of Contents.

CEC Lesson Plans

www.col-ed.org/cur/

CEC Lesson Plans, sponsored by the Columbia Education Center in Portland, Oregon, features a wide variety of lesson plans created by teachers for use in their own classrooms. To find language arts plans to fit your needs, scroll to Language Arts and click Elementary (K-5), Intermediate (6-8), or High School (9-12).

Cinderella Stories

www.acs.ucalgary.ca/~dkbrown/cinderella.html

Cinderella Stories contains lesson plans with multicultural versions of Cinderella for Grades 3-7. Scroll to Teaching Ideas by Jean Rusting where you'll find plans for Tattercoats, Cap o' Rushes, The Twelve Months, and The Princess and the Golden Shoes. You can also print a copy of these different versions.

Collaborative Lesson Archive

http://faldo.atmos.uiuc.edu/CLA/

Collaborative Lesson Archive, created by Bill and Dee Chapman, is a forum for the creation, distribution, and archiving of education curricula for all grade levels and subject areas. To find language arts lesson plans for each grade level, click the grade level you want and then select either Reading or Writing. You can also submit a lesson plan.

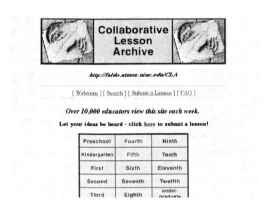

Connecting Students

www.connectingstudents.com/

Connecting Students, maintained by David Leahy, provides a collection of Internet-ready lesson plans for Grades K-12. Teachers will find language arts plans in the lesson plans, themes, Web lessons, and literacy sections.

Connections+

www.mcrel.org/resources/plus/

McREL's **Connections+** provides a collection of lesson plans and activities for Grades K-12. Click Language Arts, where you'll find plans for a variety of topics. The site also offers Haiku resources in the Multi/Inter-disciplinary section.

Curriculum Guide for the Elementary Level: English Language Arts

www.sasked.gov.sk.ca/docs/ela/ela.html

The Saskatchewan Department of Education provides a curriculum guide with more than 50 lessons for teaching English language arts in Grades 1-5. To find the Sample Units, scroll near the bottom of the page.

CyberGuides: Teacher Guides & Student Activities

www.sdcoe.k12.ca.us/score/cyberguide.html

CyberGuides: Teacher Guides & Student Activities, from the SCORE Language Arts Project, are supplementary teacher-developed units based on nearly 100 core works of literature, designed for students to use with the World Wide Web. Each CyberGuide, organized by grade level, contains a student and teacher edition, objectives, a task, and a process by which it may be completed. A rubric for assessing the quality of the student's work is also included.

EDSITEment

http://edsitement.neh.fed.us/

EDSITEment, a joint project of the National Endowment for the Humanities, the Council of the Great City Schools, MCI Communications Corp., and the National Trust for the Humanities, contains online lesson plans for teaching English, history, art history, and foreign languages at the high school level. To find them, click Lesson Plans.

Educate the Children: Lesson Plans

www.educate.org.uk/lessons.htm

Educate the Children provides a collection of hundreds of lesson plans and worksheets contributed by teachers for Grades K–12. Click English to find more than 180 lesson plans.

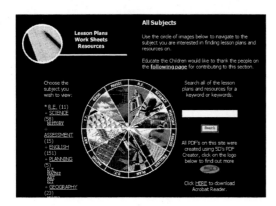

Education World: Language Arts Lesson Plans

http://db.education-world.com/perl/browse?cat_id=1874

Education World: Language Arts Lesson Plans, sponsored by American Fidelity Services, provides nearly 200 language arts lesson plans for Grades K–12. Categories include Journalism, Literature, Reading, Vocabulary, Whole Language, and Writing/Composition.

Encarta Lesson Collection

www.encarta.msn.com/schoolhouse/lessons/

Encarta Lesson Collection offers a collection of lesson plans contributed by K–12 teachers in various subject areas. To find language arts plans, click Language Arts.

Fairy Tales from Far Off Lands

www.richmond.edu/~ed344/webunits/fairytales/title.html

Fairy Tales from Far Off Lands features a collection of Internet-based lesson plans for studying fables around the world for Grades 4–6. Places and countries covered include Africa, central Asia, China, Egypt, England, native America, Russia, and Scotland.

Free Exemplary Lesson Plans

www.indiana.edu/~eric_rec/bks/lessons.html

Free Exemplary Lesson Plans, from ERIC Clearinghouse on Reading, English, and Communication, is a collection of K–12 language arts lesson plans taken from ERIC publications.

Free Online Unit Studies

www.alaska.net/~cccandc/free.htm

Free Online Unit Studies contains Charity Lovelace's language arts units on Ducks, Learning With the Little House, A Sensory Summer, and Under the Sea for the primary grades. The site also includes a collection of more than 300 other curriculum units for Grades K–8 from the Internet. To find an alphabetical index to the collection, scroll to "More Online Unit Studies."

Gareth Pitchford's Primary Resources

http://members.aol.com/garethford/GPwebpage.htm

Gareth Pitchford provides hundreds of lesson plan ideas and worksheets, including language arts resources for the primary grades.

Gateway to Educational Materials (GEM)

www.thegateway.org/

GEM, sponsored by the U.S. Department of Education, provides access to hundreds of lesson plans, curriculum units, and other education resources on the Internet for Grades K–12. To find a list of language arts plans, select Browse Subject Lists and click Language Arts.

Gryphon House, Inc.

www.ghbooks.com/

Gryphon House, Inc., provides a wealth of online language arts lessons and activities from every book the company publishes. To find a preschool and primary grade collection, select Get Free Activities! and scroll to Activity Books or Language Arts.

Homework Central: Language Arts

www.homeworkcentral.com/
highschool1.htp?sectionid=1910

Homework Central provides a collection of language arts lesson plans arranged by topic for Grades K–12. Teachers can also find other language arts plans by subject or grade level in the Lesson Plan Archives.

Jan Brett's Home Page

www.janbrett.com/

Jan Brett's Home Page, from the well-known picture book author and illustrator, provides a wealth of printable activities for primary grade students. They can make animal masks, use color pages, work on fun projects, read the "all abouts," and view lovely drawings in the Newsnotes section. Students can also send an electronic postcard from Brett's collection of more than 40 cards. In the Piggybacks section, teachers will find classroom lessons and projects to accompany some of Brett's books.

Kevin's Lesson Center

www.cbv.ns.ca/sstudies/lesson/lesson.html

Kevin's Lesson Center features a collection of lesson plans contributed by teachers for Grades 4–12. The site includes English/language arts plans.

KidReach: Lesson Plans and Activities

www.westga.edu/~kidreach/lessons.html

KidReach: Lesson Plans and Activities provides unit lesson plans contributed by student teachers for teaching literature in Grades 4–12. The site includes unit plans for the following books and plays: *Spirit Quest* by Susan Sharpe, *Daniel's Story* by Carol Matas, *Macbeth* and *Romeo and Juliet* by William Shakespeare, and *Night* by Elie Wiesel.

Kodak: Lesson Plans

www.kodak.com/edu/lessonPlans/
lessonPlans.shtml

Kodak: Lesson Plans is a collection of lesson plans that combine photography and various curricular areas for Grades K–12. The site includes nearly 60 lesson plans for language arts and English. All the plans require a camera.

Language Arts

www.csun.edu/~vceed009/languagearts.html

Language Arts, from Web Sites and Resources for Teachers, is one of the most comprehensive sites for lesson plans and other language arts resources. The site contains thousands of lesson plans, a number of online student activities, and hundreds of literature links for Grades K-12.

Learning Activities Archive

www.score.kaplan.com/activities/archive.html

Learning Activities Archive, from Kaplan's SCORE, provides a collection of lessons for various curriculum areas. Language arts topics include reading, vocabulary, grammar, creative writing, poetry, and writing a report.

Learning Resources

http://literacynet.org/cnnsf/

Learning Resources is a collection of weekly online interactive lessons using CNN news stories edited for easier reading for students in Grades 6-12. The interactive lessons for each news story include curriculum exercises to test comprehension.

Lesson Plan Place

www.inet-edu.com/lessons/links/

The Internet Education Group provides a collection of hundreds of links to thousands of lesson plans for integrating the Internet into K-12 classrooms including language arts plans.

Lesson Plans for Technology

http://fcit.coedu.usf.edu/tnt/

Lesson Plans for Technology, part of Technology 'Nformation for Teachers (T'NT), is a database of more than 250 technology-related lesson plans developed by Florida teachers for Grades 4-12. The site includes plans for language arts as well as other subject areas. Each lesson plan contains computer and subject information and provides detailed instructions on how to implement the lesson in your classroom. You can search for plans by subject area, grade level, and keyword.

Lesson Plans from National Core Knowledge Conferences

www.coreknowledge.org/CKproto2/resrcs/

Lesson Plans from National Core Knowledge Conferences is a collection of units and lesson plans developed by teachers in Core Knowledge schools for Grades PK-8. The collection contains integrated plans for a variety of subjects, including language arts.

Lesson Plans from the Teacher's Desk

www.knownet.net/users/Ackley/lessons.html

Lesson Plans from the Teacher's Desk is a collection of more than 250 of Angela Ackley's lesson ideas and activities for teaching spelling, writing, English, reading, and vocabulary in Grades 4-6.

The Lesson Plans Page

www.lessonplanspage.com/

The Lesson Plans Page, by Kyle Yamnitz, contains hundreds of lesson plans, including language arts plans, for Grades K-6.

Lesson Stop

www.lessonstop.org/

Lesson Stop, maintained by Therese Sarah, contains more than 500 sites with thousands of lesson plans for Grades K-12. The site includes language arts plans organized by topic and grade level. Other plans, such as Spinning Tales, can be found in the L.S. Lessons section.

LETSNet: Language Arts Lesson Plans

http://commtechlab.msu.edu/sites/letsnet/noframes/Subjects/la/

LETSNet: Language Arts Lesson Plans, from Learning Exchange for Teachers and Students Through the Internet, is designed for K-12 classrooms. It contains a collection of teaching units with online student activities that incorporate reading, writing, and research skills. The units include Ellis Island, Essay Exchange, School Newspaper, What's in a Name?, and Holiday Explorations.

The Library in the Sky

www.nwrel.org/sky/

The Library in the Sky, provided by Northwest Regional Educational Laboratory (NWREL), contains hundreds of K-12 lesson plans for a variety of subject areas. To find language arts plans, choose Teacher Resources, select Lesson Plans, and click Language Arts.

Linguistics 577 Lesson Plans

http://humanities.byu.edu/linguistics/lp/home.html

Linguistics 577 Lesson Plans, created by Brigham Young University students, features a variety of language arts plans, including reading, writing, and grammar, for Grades 7-12.

Link-to-Learn Classroom Activities

http://l2l.ed.psu.edu/success/l2l_indx.htm

Link-to-Learn, an initiative of the Commonwealth of Pennsylvania, contains a collection of hundreds of Internet-enriched lesson plans, units, and activities contributed by teachers for Grades K-12. Language arts teachers can find lesson plans for the elementary school, middle school, and high school. Each classroom activity includes a plan to organize and structure the lesson, an activity worksheet that can be used online or printed for use as a handout, and extension tips with related sites for the lesson.

McDougal Littell's Spelling Lessons

www.mcdougallittell.com/lit/spelling/howto.htm

McDougal Littell provides 32 online spelling lessons for Grades 6-8 that can supplement any middle school language arts curriculum. Each lesson includes a teacher's page and a student's page.

McREL: Lesson Plans and Activities

www.mcrel.org/connect/lesson.html

McREL: Lesson Plans and Activities, compiled by the Mid-Continent Regional Educational Laboratory, contains a collection of K–12 lesson plans for a variety of curricular areas. For the language arts plans and activities, click Language Arts.

Outta Ray's Head

www3.sympatico.ca/ray.saitz/

Outta Ray's Head features a collection of more than 100 language arts lesson plans containing printable handouts for teaching poetry, literature, writing, and library skills in Grades 7–12.

Penguin Putnam: Teacher's Guides

www.penguinputnam.com/academic/
resources/guides/

Penguin Putnam, suitable for high school English classes, provides Teachers' Guides for a variety of Signet classics. These printable guides contain ready-to-use lesson plans, discussion questions, and chapter-by-chapter and scene-by-scene breakdowns of numerous books used in high school English classes. For another source of plans, click Readers' Guides in the Classics section.

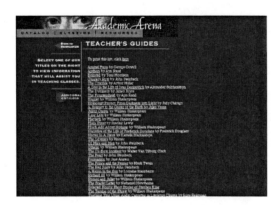

RHL School

www.rhlschool.com/

RHL School provides printable worksheets to complement language arts programs in Grades 4–8. You'll find a collection of worksheets for English basics, reading comprehension, and reference skills. Teachers can request a free answer key that is updated weekly and sent by e-mail.

Scholastic In School

www.scholastic.com/inschool/

Scholastic In School provides a collection of ready-to-use reproducible activities for reading, writing, phonics, and spelling in Grades 1–6. The worksheets include answer keys and can be used independently of Scholastic materials.

Schoolhouse: English and Language Arts

http://teacherpathfinder.org/School/
english.html

Schoolhouse: English and Language Arts, part of Teacher/Pathfinder, provides a collection of English/language arts lesson plans for reading and writing in Grades K–12. You can also search the site for lesson plans.

Scripps Howard National Spelling Bee

www.spellingbee.com/studyact.htm

Scripps Howard National Spelling Bee offers an entire year's worth of vocabulary activities, tips, and spelling lessons for Grades 4–8. To find this material, click Mrs. Brooks' Lesson Plans and Carolyn's Corner in the Study Activities and Tips section.

The Shakespeare Corner

www.bell.k12.ca.us/BellHS/Littauer/
Shakespeare.Corner

The Shakespeare Corner, created by Joel Littauer, contains lesson plans for teaching units on William Shakespeare's *Romeo and Juliet* in Grade 9, *Julius Caesar* in Grade 10, and *Hamlet* in Grade 12. Each unit includes a teacher's guide, online student activities, and links to related sites.

Story House Bound Books

www.story-house.com/

Story House Bound Books, for Grades 1-7, contains teachers' guides for a wide variety of books ranging from *Arthur Meets the President* to *The Titanic Lost ... And Found* to *Walk Two Moons*. Each book is briefly described. In addition, the site offers other free teachers' guides in the Teachers Resources section.

Surfing with the Bard: Lesson Plans

www.ulen.com/shakespeare/teachers/lessons/
lessons.html

Amy Ulen provides more than 40 lesson plans for teaching Shakespeare to high school classes. Included are plans for *Hamlet*, *As You Like It*, *Macbeth*, *A Midsummer Night's Dream*, *Romeo & Juliet*, and other plays.

SurLaLune Fairy Tale Pages

http://members.aol.com/surlalune/frytales/

SurLaLune Fairy Tale Pages is a collection of annotated fairy tales, including histories, biographies, and comparisons between similar tales. The site is suitable for Grades 4-7.

Teacher Guide!

www.cagle.com/teacher/

Teacher Guide! features online lesson plans that use an extensive collection of current editorial cartoons from newspapers around the country. The site includes plans with printable student handouts for elementary school, middle school, and high school students in various subject areas, including English and journalism.

Teacher Talk Forum

http://education.indiana.edu/cas/ttforum/
lesson.html

Teacher Talk Forum, sponsored by the Center for Adolescent Studies at the Indiana University School of Education, provides a collection of electronic lesson plans covering a variety of topic areas for Grades 7-12. To find language arts plans, scroll and click Language Arts.

Teachers Helping Teachers

www.pacificnet.net/~mandel/LanguageArts.html

Teachers Helping Teachers, updated weekly, is a forum where K-12 teachers can share lesson plans in language arts and other subject areas. Teachers can also find classroom management ideas and a topic-of-the-week feature by clicking Teachers Helping Teachers Home Page at the bottom of the page.

Teachers.Net Lesson Bank

http://teachers.net/lessons/

The **Teachers.Net Lesson Bank**, a curriculum exchange forum for Grades PK–12, provides a searchable collection of more than 400 lesson plans and activities contributed by teachers. To find language arts lesson plans, click Reading/Writing or Literature on the left side, or Curricula at the top of the page.

TeachersFirst Web Content Matrix

www.teachersfirst.com/matrix-f.htm

TeachersFirst Web Content Matrix, provided by the Network for Instructional Television (NITV), offers a collection of lesson plans at the elementary, middle, and high school levels. To find language arts plans, scroll to Literature & Reading or Writing in the table and click lesson plans.

Teaching Ideas for Primary Teachers

www.warner.clara.net/

Teaching Ideas for Primary Teachers, created by Mark Warner, contains a collection of English and time-filler activities to complement a K–5 language arts curriculum. The site also includes worksheets that can be printed and photocopied for classroom use.

Teaching Shakespeare

www.folger.edu/education/

Teaching Shakespeare, sponsored by the Folger Shakespeare Library in Washington, D.C., contains a collection of lesson plans contributed by classroom teachers for Grades 8–12. The plans cover a variety of plays and ideas.

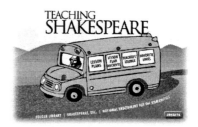

Teaching Shakespeare

Since 1984, the Folger Shakespeare Library has held ten *Teaching Shakespeare* Institutes, funded by the National Endowment for the Humanities. These Institutes bring together some of the country's most talented teachers with scholars, master teachers, and actors and offer classroom teachers the opportunity to research in the world's foremost Shakespeare collection. The 1998 Institute focused specifically on disseminating that research world-wide. The lesson plans that you'll find in this site represent the best of the teachers' work over the summer, tested and refined in the classroom during the school year.

Teachnet.Com

www.teachnet.com/

Teachnet.Com designed by teachers for K–12 teachers, offers language arts lesson ideas for reading, writing, terminology, and general areas.

TEAMS Distance Learning: K–12 Lesson Plans

http://teams.lacoe.edu/documentation/places/lessons.html

TEAMS Distance Learning: K–12 Lesson Plans, maintained by the Los Angeles County Office of Education, provides a collection of lessons plan sites for Grades K–12 organized by subject. To find language arts lesson plans, click Language Arts. You'll also find more language arts plans in the Multi-Subject Lesson Plans collection.

Tried n True Model Lesson Plans

www.teachers-connect.net/TNT/

Tried n True Model Lesson Plans, from the North Carolina Department of Public Instruction, is a collection of K-12 lesson plans contributed by teachers for a variety of subject areas. To find language arts plans, select a grade level and click the English Language Arts key in the table.

World School

www.wvaworldschool.org/

World School, created by the West Virginia Department of Education, provides a collection of Internet-based lesson plans developed by teachers for Grades K-12. Among the lesson plans are language arts, including an alphabetical list of literature units.

The Write Site

www.writesite.org/

The Write Site, developed by Greater Dayton Public Television for the middle school language arts curriculum, has students take the role of reporters and editors to research, write, and publish their own newspapers. The site includes unit outlines, student handouts, exercises, information on how to write materials, and much more.

WritingDEN

www2.actden.com/writ_den/

WritingDEN provides interactive online reading, comprehension, and writing lessons for students in Grades 6-12. Using RealAudio, students can hear words pronounced and sentences narrated. The site, updated weekly, includes a teacher's guide, an archive of more topics, a grammar guide in the tips-o-matic section, an e-mail word-of-the-day feature, and a message board where students can post their messages.

Yale-New Haven Teachers Institute

www.cis.yale.edu/ynhti/

The **Yale-New Haven Teachers Institute** offers a collection of hundreds of curriculum units for Grades K-12 prepared by teachers attending summer workshops from 1978 to 1997. Many of the units include lesson plans, student handouts, and specific classroom ideas. You can find language arts units by clicking Curricular Resources.

A & E Biography Find

www.biography.com/find/find.html

A & E Biography Find offers a searchable and browsable biography database of more than 20,000 of the greatest names, past and present, at your fingertips. Click a letter or enter a name in the box to discover who an individual is, what he or she did, and why. The site is suitable for Grades 5-12.

About.com's Mark Twain

http://marktwain.miningco.com/

About.com's Mark Twain, maintained by Jim Zwick, provides a wide-ranging compilation of material by and about Twain. To find classroom materials for Grades 8-12, click Teaching Resources. For a list of all the site's resources, click Net Links.

Aesop's Fables

www.pacificnet.net/~johnr/aesop/

Aesop's Fables, created by John R. Long, contains an alphabetically arranged collection of more than 650 fables for Grades 4-12. Nearly half of them are presented on RealAudio, and the moral is explained for all of the fables.

Aha! Poetry

www.ahapoetry.com/

Aha! Poetry provides a wide variety of online poetry resources for Grades 4-12. Students can learn poetic forms, such as cinquain, ghazal, renga, sijo, and tanka. They can also add lines or commentary to existing poems in Ann Cantelow's interactive poetry pages, or post their own poems.

Author Pages on the WWW

http://falcon.jmu.edu/~ramseyil/author.htm

Author Pages on the WWW provides a comprehensive collection of author sites, compiled by Inez Ramsey, for Grades 6-12. Categories consist of general resources, poet pages, women authors, young adult authors, individual author pages, and women authors from Mexico.

Awesome Cyber Greeting Cards

www.marlo.com/card.htm

Awesome Cyber Greeting Cards provides a large catalog of free online greeting cards you can personalize and send by e-mail in a matter of seconds. Card categories include all-occasions, holiday, award, birthday, thank you, kids, baby, and graduation. The site is suitable for students in Grades 4-12.

Baker Street Connection

www.citsoft.com/holmes.html

Baker Street Connection features a collection of Sherlock Holmes-related material, including the complete canon of 56 stories and four novels written by Sir Arthur Conan Doyle between 1887 and 1925. The site is suitable for Grades 8-12.

Barr's English Class

www.capecod.net/~bbarsant/class/

Barr's English Class, created by Nantucket High School teacher Robert P. Barsanti, contains his own class handouts, student worksheets, creative writing, and essay tips as well as related sites for teaching more than 40 literary works in Grades 9-12.

The Book Review Forum

http://faldo.atmos.uiuc.edu/BOOKREVIEW/

The Book Review Forum, created by Bill Chapman for elementary school students, features a list of book reviews written by students for other students. Students rate books they really want to read! To send a review, students can click Submit a Book Review and follow the online directions. They can also post a follow-up to a book already reviewed.

Books.com's Contents

www.books.com/scripts/browse.exe?

Books.com's Contents offers the Author's Pen section, which contains biographical information, author photos, and links to home pages for more than 1,000 authors. You'll also find the Hall of Fame for the various prestigious book awards and an Electronic Library with thousands of copyright-free books online. In the Specialty Bookstores section, you'll find monthly book reviews, including children's book reviews. The site is suitable for Grades K-12.

Booktalks—Quick and Simple

www.concord.k12.nh.us/schools/rundlett/ booktalks

Booktalks—Quick and Simple, maintained by Rundlett Middle School in Concord, New Hampshire, is a database of more than 650 short booktalks for introducing books to students in Grades K-12. You can view the short reviews by author index or title index.

The Children's Literature Web Guide

www.acs.ucalgary.ca/~dkbrown/

The Children's Literature Web Guide, maintained by David K. Brown, is one of the premier comprehensive resources for teaching children's literature in the elementary school. The site provides online children's stories, general children's literature resources, book awards, teacher resources, links to individual author sites, and much, much more.

Classic Short Stories

www.bnl.com/shorts/

Classic Short Stories, collected by Gary Lindquist for Grades 8-12, contains an online anthology of short stories and links to related sites. Stories range from "Young Goodman Brown" by Nathaniel Hawthorne to "The Use of Force" by William Carlos Williams to "The Pit and the Pendulum" by Edgar Allan Poe.

ClueMaster

www.cluemaster.com/

ClueMaster, a free subscription service for Grades 5-12, offers a collection of hundreds of crossword puzzles, word searches, and other word games that can be printed from your browser. The 50 quick crosswords and word searches are suitable for younger students, while the more challenging cryptic crosswords are suitable for high school students. Each word puzzle includes a printable answer sheet.

Cool Word of the Day

www.edu.yorku.ca/~wotd

Cool Word of the Day, presented by York University College of Education in Canada, is a good way for students in Grades 5-12 to build their English vocabularies. The site provides a new word daily, its definition, and an archive of past words.

Debbie's Unit Factory

www.themeunits.com/

Debbie's Unit Factory contains a collection of cross-curricular units and online resources for enriching language arts teaching in the elementary school. Click Table of Contents to find a list of the theme units, including free sample material and online quizzes. To find topical and monthly links, click Sneak Peeks.

The Dickens Page

http://lang.nagoya-u.ac.jp/~matsuoka/Dickens.html

The Dickens Page, maintained by Mitsuharu Matsuoka, contains a vast collection of sites devoted to Charles Dickens. Included are photos, biographical information, electronic texts, recreational and film information, and other resources.

Emily Dickinson Random Epigram Machine

www.io.com/~smith/ed/

The **Emily Dickinson Random Epigram Machine** generates, every time you reload the page, a different Emily Dickinson poem. The poems are from *The Complete Poems of Emily Dickinson*, edited by Thomas Johnson, and *New Poems of Emily Dickinson*, edited by William H. Schurr. The site is suitable for Grades 7-12.

ePALS Classroom Exchange

www.epals.com/

ePALS Classroom Exchange, available in English, Spanish, or French for Grades K-12, connects nearly 14,000 classrooms from 100 countries around the world. You can search the site's database by school name, the classroom's first language, grade, the city/town, state/province, or country. You can then send an e-mail or visit the school's home page to find out if a student there would like to become your pen pal.

The Encyclopedia Mythica

www.pantheon.org/mythica/

The Encyclopedia Mythica is an extensive encyclopedia of articles dealing with mythology, folklore, and legends from many the world's cultures. It contains more than 5,000 definitions of gods and goddesses, supernatural beings, and legendary creatures and monsters. The site is suitable for Grades 6-12.

The English Server

http://eserver.org/

The English Server, from Carnegie Mellon University, is a cooperative that has been publishing humanities texts online since 1990. Today it offers more than 20,000 works covering a wide range of interests for K-12 language arts teachers.

ERIC/REC Clearinghouse

www.indiana.edu/~eric_rec/

ERIC/REC Clearinghouse is dedicated to providing reading, English, and communication (REC) educational materials, services, and course work to anyone interested in the language arts. The site is suitable for Grades K-12.

Fairrosa Cyber Library

www.users.interport.net/~fairrosa/

Fairrosa Cyber Library features an online reading room with bookshelves of classics, fairy tales and folk tales, and stories and rhymes for students in Grades K-8. The site also contains a Lewis Carroll collection, an annotated list of dragon stories, an index to popular children's authors and illustrators, and related links to children's literature.

Fake Out!

www.eduplace.com/dictionary/

Fake Out!, provided by Houghton Mifflin for Grades K-8, is a weekly definition guessing game in which a student selects a word from a grade-level list and tries to match it with its definition. The site includes answers, an archive of previous words, and teaching suggestions. Students can also choose one of next week's words, write their own fake definitions, and e-mail the definitions.

Fluency Through Fables

www.comenius.com/fables/

Fluency Through Fables, presented by the Comenius Group, offers a new short fable every two months. Each fable is accompanied by a variety of online, interactive, self-correcting comprehension and vocabulary exercises. The site is suitable for Grades 5-12.

Grammar Now!

www.grammarnow.com/

Grammar Now!, answers any grammar, usage, composition, or editing question you have by e-mail. The site, suitable for Grades 6-12, provides a convenient form to e-mail your questions and includes other useful grammar sites.

Granddad's Animal Book

www.maui.com/~twright/animals/alphabet.htm

Granddad's Animal Book, created by Thomas Wright for primary grade students, is an online interactive book that has a rhyme and an animal picture for each letter of the English alphabet. Clicking an animal takes you to a page with an illustration, a couplet, and some information on the species shown, plus links to other pertinent sites.

Grandpa Tucker's Rhymes and Tales

www.night.net/tucker/

Grandpa Tucker's Rhymes and Tales, updated monthly, features a collection of short, silly poems and online humorous stories written in verse for elementary school kids. The site also offers tips and materials for teaching poetry in the Family Fun Rhyme Time section. Teachers can print out the poetry to use in their own classrooms.

Great Writers and Poets

www.xs4all.nl/~pwessel/writers.html

Great Writers and Poets, part of the Book Lovers home page, offers an alphabetized collection of prize-winning author sites as well as other author sites for high school English. Each author site includes a brief biography, short reviews of the major works, sample writings, a photo, and related links.

Grimm's Fairy Tales

www.cs.cmu.edu/~spok/grimmtmp/

Grimm's Fairy Tales, for Grades K–5, provides a complete online collection of the 209 fairy tales written by the brothers Grimm. Translations are by Margaret Hunt.

Guide to Grammar and Writing

http://webster.commnet.edu/HP/pages/darling/grammar.htm

Guide to Grammar and Writing, prepared by Charles Darling, is a comprehensive grammar reference for high school students. The site contains 38 computer-graded, cleverly animated quizzes that test a student's knowledge of grammar. Students can click grandma's rocker to Ask Grammar a question about punctuation, word usage, writing, or other related topics. A special form appears on which students can submit their questions. For hundreds of previously answered questions on grammar, click Grammar Logs.

Hans Christian Andersen Fairy Tales and Stories

www.math.technion.ac.il/~rl/Andersen/

Hans Christian Andersen Fairy Tales and Stories, compiled by Zvi Har'El for Grades K–5, contains the complete list of Andersen's 168 stories in the chronological order of their original publication.

Home Page for Hamlet and Macbeth

www.webcom.com/falcon/

Home Page for Hamlet and Macbeth, sponsored by Falcon Education Link, makes the study of Shakespeare more enjoyable and understandable for high school students. Rodger Burnich, an English teacher, wrote the guides to *Hamlet* and *Macbeth*. The site also includes related Shakespeare links.

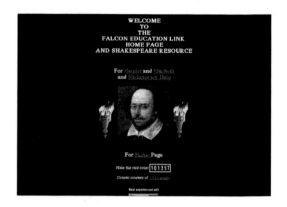

Index of Shakespeare Plays

www.unc.edu/~monroem/shakespeare/shakespeare.html

Index of Shakespeare Plays contains Matthew Monroe's summaries of plots for all 37 of Shakespeare's plays. Each summary covers the major developments and most of the important characters in the play. The material is useful for students in Grades 7–12.

International Reading Association

www.reading.org/

International Reading Association (IRA) provides leadership in promoting literacy, improving the quality of reading instruction and teaching techniques, serving as a clearinghouse for the dissemination of reading research, and encouraging the lifetime reading habit. The site is suitable for Grades K–12.

Jane Austen Information Page

www.pemberley.com/janeinfo/janeinfo.html

Jane Austen Information Page, created by Henry Churchyard, is the premiere Austen site on the Internet. It contains six full-text, annotated versions of her novels, including an illustrated version of *Pride and Prejudice*. The site, suitable for high school English classes, includes articles on and by Jane Austen, numerous photos, information on the life and times of this celebrated author, online discussions of film and TV versions of her novels, and other related pages.

John's Word Search Puzzles

www.thepotters.com/puzzles.html

John's Word Search Puzzles, updated monthly, is a collection of more than 125 printable word searches for Grades 3–8. Puzzle categories include Kids, Cities and States, Holidays Puzzles, Sports, and TV and Movies.

Kid Crosswords and Other Puzzles

www.kidcrosswords.com/

Kid Crosswords and Other Puzzles, from Brian Goss, is updated monthly and features a collection of more than 100 printable crosswords and other puzzles for various curricular areas for Grades 3–12. To find previous English, literature, and holiday puzzles, click Catalog.

KidPub

www.kidpub.org/kidpub/

KidPub contains more than 30,000 original stories written by kids from all over the world. The site provides a handy story form for submitting stories for publication. In addition, the site contains a keypals database where kids can sign up or hook up with one of the 23,000 keypals.

Kids' Books

www.scpl.lib.fl.us/kids/kids_booklists.html

The Seminole County Public Library System Services (SCPLS) in central Florida provides a collection of recommended books for students in Grades K-12. Categories range from scary stories to U.S. historical fiction. Students are invited to write a review of a book on the list that they've read, which will be published at this site. To read reviews sent in by other kids from all over the world, click the Review Index.

Kids' Space Connection: Penpal Box

www.ks-connection.com/penpal/penpal.html

Kids' Space Connection: Penpal Box provides a collection of pen pal boxes that list kids who are looking for pen pals by age group. There's a pen pal box for ages 6 and younger, ages 7 and 8, ages 9 and 10, ages 11 and 12, and ages 13 through 16. For each child, you'll find the name, nickname, e-mail address, age, country, and short bio. There's also a class box for schools and an archive of the most recent pen pal members.

Learning Train

www.thepotters.com/ltrain.html

Learning Train features activities from Building Blocks to Reading, as well as other readiness reading ideas for students in Grades PK-2.

Literary Calendar

http://litcal.yasuda-u.ac.jp/LitCalendar.shtml

Literary Calendar contains a monthly calendar of events, allowing you to click a date to see what important literary events have occurred. You can also search for literary information by names, short phrases, or dates. Many events include links to related resources. The site is suitable for Grades 8–12.

Little Explorers

www.LittleExplorers.com/Dictionary.html

Little Explorers, also available in Spanish, French, German, and Portuguese versions, is an online picture dictionary containing more than 1,200 entries and related Web sites for preschoolers and elementary students. Click a letter in the alphabet at the top of the window to see a page of words that start with that letter. You can also listen to the names of letters.

Luminarium

www.luminarium.org/lumina.htm

Luminarium contains a selection of the major English authors and their works from the medieval (1350–1485), Renaissance (1485–1603), and early 17th-century (1603–1660) periods. Each period includes an index of electronic texts, biographical information, beautiful images, a bibliography, essays and articles, and related sites. The site is suitable for high school AP English classes.

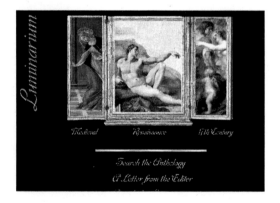

Merriam-Webster Online

www.m-w.com/

Merriam-Webster Online provides a treasury of daily word games and interactive activities for students in Grades 3-12. The site's major feature is the WWWebster Dictionary in which you can look up the meanings of more than 180,000 words and the WWWebster Thesaurus in which you can find words with similar or opposite meanings. A new feature, Word Central, is designed for the younger kids. It offers a special student dictionary, daily buzzword, and other games.

Mr. William Shakespeare and the Internet

http://daphne.palomar.edu/shakespeare/

Mr. William Shakespeare and the Internet is an annotated guide to Shakespeare resources compiled by Terry A. Gray. Sections include information on Shakespeare's works, life and times, theater, criticism, and Renaissance sources. In addition, the Shakespeare in Education section provides a collection of teaching aids for middle and high school classrooms.

My Hero

www.myhero.com/

My Hero celebrates the unsung heroes among us by asking elementary and middle school students to write about a very special person who has shown acts of courage, kindness, generosity, or ability. The site provides a Guest Book section in which students are given step-by-step instructions for submitting a description of their heroes. Students can also read about famous historical figures and ordinary heroes by scrolling and clicking on Hero Stories.

Nathaniel Hawthorne

http://eldred.ne.mediaone.net/nh/
hawthorne.html

Nathaniel Hawthorne is a Web site that contains a comprehensive collection of Hawthorne resources for high school students and teachers. The site includes electronic texts of Hawthorne's books and other writings, information about his life and work, and links to sites for other famous 19th-century American writers.

National Council of Teachers of English

www.ncte.org/

National Council of Teachers of English (NCTE) is the leading professional organization for improving the teaching of English and language arts at all grade levels. The NCTE site presents relevant information of value to K-12 classroom teachers.

Nursery Rhymes

http://members.xoom.com/nur_rhymes/

Tracy Lightfoot provides an online alphabetical list of the traditional nursery rhymes that form a large part of our childhood experiences. Rhymes marked with an asterisk provide information about their origins or interpretations. The site is suitable for Grades K-8.

The On-Line Books Page

www.cs.cmu.edu/books.html

The On-Line Books Page, from Carnegie Mellon, is a searchable and browsable database to more than 9,000 online books and links to repositories of books. The site is suitable for Grades 7-12.

PAL: Perspectives in American Literature

www.csustan.edu/english/reuben/pal/
TABLE.HTML

PAL: Perspectives in American Literature, created by Paul P. Reuben of California State University at Stanislaus, is an online research and reference guide to the major movements and authors in American literature. The site, suitable for AP English students, also provides research topics and study questions for every chapter in the guide.

PBS Kids

www.pbs.org/kids/

PBS Kids, for Grades PK-5, contains a list of links to information on PBS TV kids' shows, including the time to watch them on more than 300 local PBS stations. The site also provides a wide variety of activities in the Goodies section, including the Coloring Book, with more than 50 printable pages of favorite PBS characters.

Poetry for Kids

www.poetry4kids.com/

Poetry for Kids, for Grades K-5, contains a collection of more than 40 wonderfully funny original poems written by Kenn Nesbitt. The site also includes links to other fun poetry pages.

Poets' Corner

www.geocities.com/~spanoudi/poems/

Steve Spandouis' **Poets' Corner** contains a collection of more than 5,000 poems by more than 600 poets categorized by author. The poems ranges from medieval English ballads to poems of the early 20th century. The site is suitable for Grades K-12.

Project Bartleby Archive

www.columbia.edu/acis/bartleby/

Project Bartleby Archive, from Columbia University, features an electronic library of the major British and American authors. The site, for Grades 8-12, includes biographical information, illustrations, and online versions of the authors' works.

Purdue Online Writing Lab

http://owl.english.purdue.edu/

Purdue Online Writing Lab (OWL) features a collection of 130 handouts that students in Grades 8-12 can use to improve their writing skills. Topics include punctuation, parts of speech, correct sentence structure, spelling, and research papers. For a complete list of the topics, click Summaries in the Resources for Writers section. OWL also provides an extensive list of other online writing resources.

Reader's Theater Editions

www.aaronshep.com/rt/RTE.html

Reader's Theater Editions provides 17 short scripts adapted from stories by Aaron Shepard and others. The material is mostly humor, fantasy, and retold tales from a variety of cultures. The site also provides tips on using the scripts. Teachers in Grades 3-9 are encouraged to copy, share, and perform the scripts in their classrooms.

SCORE Language Arts

www.sdcoe.k12.ca.us/score/cla.html

SCORE Language Arts, from Schools of California Online Resources for Education, reflects the California English Language Arts Framework for the K-12 curriculum. The site provides online student projects, lessons plans, teacher resources, and much more.

The Shakespeare Classroom

www.jetlink.net/~massij/shakes/

The Shakespeare Classroom, maintained by Professor J.M. Massi, features a variety of online resources for teaching Shakespeare in high school. The materials include study questions for more than 30 of Shakespeare's plays, answers to frequently asked questions about Shakespeare and his plays, information on the filmed versions of Shakespeare's plays, and links to related Shakespeare sites.

The Shiki Internet Haiku Salon

http://cc.matsuyama-u.ac.jp/~shiki/

The Shiki Internet Haiku Salon introduces a new style of haiku poetry that has become popular in American schools. The site includes biographical information about Shiki Masaoka, anthologies of haiku, lessons on how to write haiku, and related links.

Story Creations

www.searsportrait.com/storybook/

Story Creations, provided by Sears Portrait Studio, is a collection of online, interactive stories that elementary school students can personalize by answering a few short questions. They can also print out or e-mail their stories to share with their classmates.

StoryFun!

www.mit.edu/storyfun/

StoryFun! contains online madlibs on a variety of topics. To create a hilarious story, choose a topic and type in funny verbs, nouns, and modifiers. Click the List of Story Topics to view the collection and click new story topic to reload for a new form. The material is suitable for students in Grades 6-12.

Superteach

http://nz.com/webnz/checkers/free2.html

Superteach offers a collection of online, self-correcting language arts exercises for students in Grades 6-12. Among these are the current grammar and proofreading lessons, with an archive of past grammar and proofreading lessons also available. The site includes exercises for improving a student's knowledge of idiom and slang and exercises for correcting writing mistakes.

Tales of Wonder

http://darsie.ucdavis.edu/tales/

Tales of Wonder, compiled by Richard Darsie for Grades 3-8, is a collection of more than 80 folk and fairy tales from around the world. The stories provide insight about the traditions and feelings of many cultures.

TEAMS Distance Learning

http://teams.lacoe.edu/

TEAMS Distance Learning, from the Los Angeles County Office of Education, provides a wealth of online resources of interest to K-12 language arts teachers and students.

Wacky Web Tales

www.eduplace.com/tales/

Wacky Web Tales, from Houghton Mifflin, asks students to fill in parts of speech to create wacky tales (madlibs) online. For a collection of previous tales, click More Tales. To find tales written by student writers, scroll to Choose One of Your Tales. Students can also submit their own wacky tales by e-mail. The site is suitable for Grades 4-8.

Wild World of Words Challenges

www.ash.udel.edu/ash/challenge/word.html

Wild World of Words Challenges provides a variety of interactive word games with which middle school students can improve their vocabulary, spelling, and grammar skills. Students can do online word scrambles, anagrams, and other word puzzles. They can also figure out crazy word combinations, learn new puns, and correct misspellings.

Words and Language

http://family.go.com/Categories/Activities/
Features/family_0401_02/dony/donytv_words/
donytv004.html

Words and Language, adapted from Steve and Ruth Bennett's book *365 TV-Free Activities You Can Do With Your Child*, contains an extensive collection of ready-to-use language arts activities for Grades K–6. Among the activities are a backwards spelling bee, family historian, letter exchange, rhyming game, and wordgrams.

The Wordsmyth English Dictionary-Thesaurus

www.lightlink.com/bobp/wedt/

The Wordsmyth English Dictionary-Thesaurus, developed at the University of Chicago, is an online English dictionary with a built-in thesaurus for Grades 6–12. The site also contains an S.A.T. dictionary with the 2,000 words that appear most frequently on the S.A.T. tests. There is also an English/Spanish dictionary with more than 4,000 entries, including an example sentence illustrating the meaning of each word.

Your Quotation Center

www.cyber-nation.com/victory/quotations/

Your Quotation Center, created by Cyber Nation International, features a searchable database of more than 13,000 quotes from famous people. You can view alphabetical lists of quotes by author or by subject. The site, suitable for Grades 6-12, offers to send a daily quote by e-mail.

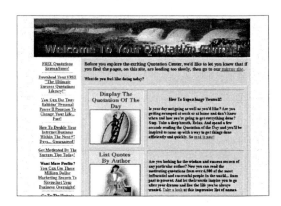

Math

The Academy Curriculum Exchange

http://ofcn.org/cyber.serv/academy/ace/

The Academy Curriculum Exchange offers lesson plans for Grades K-12 in a variety of subject areas. To find more than 50 plans for math, click these links: Elementary School, Intermediate School, or High School.

ACCESS INDIANA Teaching & Learning Center

http://tlc.ai.org/

The **ACCESS INDIANA Teaching & Learning Center** provides a collection of language arts lesson plans for Grades K-12. To find them, click **Teacher Lesson Plans** in the Mathematics section.

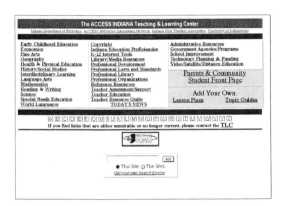

AskERIC Lesson Plans

http://ericir.syr.edu/Virtual/Lessons/Mathematics/

AskERIC Lesson Plans provides a collection of math lesson plans contributed by teachers for Grades K-12. Topics include Algebra, Applied Math, Arithmetic, Functions, Geometry, Measurement, and Probability. Each lesson plan features an overview, purpose, objectives, activities, and resource materials.

ASPECT Activities

www.bgsu.edu/colleges/edhd/programs/ASPECT/activity.html

The **Assessment Project for Erie County Teachers (ASPECT)** provides a collection of lesson plans organized by grade level for Grades K-12. Most of the plans include reproducible student worksheets.

The Awesome Library: Math Lesson Plans

www.neat-schoolhouse.org/Library/Materials_Search/Lesson_Plans/Math.html

The Awesome Library: Math Lesson Plans contains a collection of hundreds of math lesson plans for Grades K-12.

Big Sky Math Gopher Menu

gopher://bvsd.k12.co.us:70/11/Educational_Resources/Lesson_Plans/Big%20Sky/math

Big Sky Math Gopher Menu presents math lesson plans for K-12 classes. It includes a large collection for teaching a variety of topics, including fractions, decimals, whole numbers, ratios, and story problems.

CEC Lesson Plans

www.col-ed.org/cur/

CEC Lesson Plans, sponsored by the Columbia Education Center in Portland, Oregon, features a wide variety of lesson plans created by teachers for use in their own classrooms. To find math plans to fit your needs, scroll to Mathematics and click Elementary (K-5), Intermediate (6-8), or High School (9-12).

Conjectures in Geometry

www.geom.umn.edu/~dwiggins/mainpage.html

Conjectures in Geometry from the University of Minnesota's Geometry Center contains interactive lessons featuring 20 conjectures found in typical geometry texts. Included in each conjecture are definitions, sketches and explanations, SketchPad demonstrations, and follow-up activities with solutions.

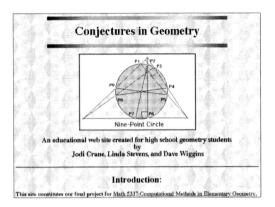

Connections+

www.mcrel.org/resources/plus/

Connections+ consists of Internet resources—lesson plans, activities, and curriculum resources—provided by Mid-Continent Regional Educational Laboratory (McREL). K–12 math teachers can select from among these topics: Calculators, Patterns, Fractals, Computers, Functions, Algebra, and Polyhedra.

CRPC GirlTECH Lesson Plans

www.crpc.rice.edu/CRPC/Women/GirlTECH/Lessons/

The **Center for Research on Parallel Computation (CRPC)** provides a collection of more than 80 GirlTECH Internet-based lesson plans dating back to 1995. The lessons, contributed by teachers for middle and high school students, cover a wide variety of math topics.

Cynthia Lanius' Mathematics Lessons

http://math.rice.edu/~lanius/Lessons/

Cynthia Lanius provides a collection of her own 15 math lessons for Grades 6-12. Lessons include math puzzles as well as algebra and geometry problems.

Educate the Children: Lesson Plans

www.educate.org.uk/lessons.htm

Educate the Children provides a collection of hundreds of lesson plans and worksheets contributed by teachers for Grades K-12. Click Math to find more than 100 lesson plans.

Education World: Math Lesson Plans

http://db.education-world.com/perl/browse?cat_id=1875

Education World: Math Lesson Plans, sponsored by American Fidelity Services, provides nearly 400 math lesson plans for Grades K-12. Categories include Algebra, Applied Mathematics, Arithmetic, Geometry, Measurement, and Probability.

Encarta Lesson Collection

www.encarta.msn.com/schoolhouse/lessons/

Encarta Lesson Collection offers a collection of lesson plans contributed by K-12 teachers in various subject areas. To find mathematics plans, click Mathematics.

Explorer

http://explorer.scrtec.org/explorer/

Explorer is a mammoth collection of math lesson plans and activities for K–12 classes. Click Mathematics Folders to find a variety of plans on many topics, including problem solving and reasoning, whole numbers and numeration, geometry, algebraic ideas, and measurement.

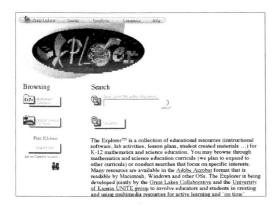

Forum Web Units and Lessons

http://forum.swarthmore.edu/web.units.html

Forum Web Units and Lessons is a collection of Internet-based projects with lesson materials for Grades 6–12. Among the projects are Tom Scavo's "Adventures in Statistics and Tangrams," Richard Briston's "Tenth Grade Internet Math Assignments," Norman Shapiro's "Geometry Through Art," Jan Garner's "Perspective Drawing, Moebius Strip, Polyhedra, and Spreadsheets," and Suzanne Alejandre's "Polyhedra in the Classroom and Tessellation Tutorials."

Frank Potter's Science Gems— Mathematics

www-sci.lib.uci.edu/SEP/math.html

Frank Potter's Science Gems—Mathematics provides an exhaustive collection of K–12 lesson plans and activities sorted into 23 math categories.

Gareth Pitchford's Primary Resources

http://members.aol.com/garethford/
GPwebpage.htm

Gareth Pitchford provides hundreds of lesson plan ideas and worksheets, including math resources for the primary grades.

Gateway to Educational Materials (GEM)

www.thegateway.org/

GEM, sponsored by the U.S. Department of Education, provides access to hundreds of lesson plans, curriculum units, and other education resources on the Internet for Grades K–12. To find a list of mathematics plans, select Browse Subject Lists and click Mathematics.

Good News Bears Stock Market Project

www.ncsa.uiuc.edu/edu/RSE/RSEyellow/
gnb.html

Good News Bears Stock Market Project is an interdisciplinary unit specifically designed for middle school math students and teachers. It revolves around an interactive stock market competition in which students use real-time stock market data from the New York Stock Exchange and NASDAQ. The unit includes lesson plans and activities, reproducible pages, student handouts, and other related teaching materials.

Hands-on Math: Activities for the Elementary Classroom

www.xmission.com/~dparker/mathpage/handson.html

Janine Parker's **Hands-on Math: Activities for the Elementary Classroom** contains classroom-tested lesson plans in geometry, number patterns, and topology. The geometry plans include step-by-step instructions for constructing the Platonic solids out of toothpicks and gumdrops.

Houghton Mifflin Activity Search

www.eduplace.com/search/activity2.html

Houghton Mifflin Activity Search features a searchable curriculum database in which K-8 teachers can find math lesson plans by grade level. Activities can also be browsed by theme.

Internet Mathematics Library

http://forum.swarthmore.edu/library/resource_types/lesson_plans/

The Math Forum provides hundreds of mathematics lesson plans selected from the Internet collections and individual author sites for Grades K-12. The searchable and browsable collection is sorted by topic and grade level.

K–12 Statistics

www.mste.uiuc.edu/stat/stat.html

K–12 Statistics contains a list of Internet-based statistics lessons. The lessons include the following topics: NCAA basketball finals, earthquakes, minimum-maximum temperatures, weather plots, and temperatures.

KQED/CELL Math Lessons

www.kqed.org/cell/school/math/mathonline/lessons/

KQED/CELL Math Lessons, sponsored by KQED's Center for Education and Lifelong Learning (CELL), presents a series of cross-curricular math lessons for K-12 students and teachers. The lessons, organized by grade level, feature KQED and other online lessons, including video resources produced by public broadcasting for Northern California. Teachers can use many of the lessons without the videos.

The Lesson Plans Page

www.lessonplanspage.com/

The Lesson Plans Page, by Kyle Yamnitz, contains hundreds of lesson plans, including math for Grades K-6.

The Library in the Sky

www.nwrel.org/sky/

The Library in the Sky, provided by Northwest Regional Educational Laboratory (NWREL), contains hundreds of K-12 lesson plans for a variety of subject areas. To find mathematics plans, choose Teacher Resources, select Lesson Plans, and click Math.

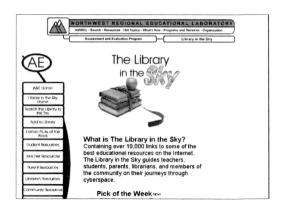

Math

www.csun.edu/~vceed009/math.html

Math contains a wide variety of math sites for lesson plans, online activities, and other math resources.

Mathematic Strategies Lesson Plans

www.dpi.state.nc.us/Curriculum/Mathematics/MathMatrix.html

Mathematic Strategies Lesson Plans, from the North Carolina Department of Public Instruction, provides a collection of mathematic strategies to match math competency goals in Grades 1, 2, and 4. To find a math lesson, select a double X in the table and click a mathematic strategy.

Mathematics Archives: K–12 Teaching Materials

http://archives.math.utk.edu/k12.html

Mathematics Archives: K–12 Teaching Materials contains extensive collections of lesson plans, activities, and other Internet resources for teaching K–12 math.

Mathematics Lessons Database

www.mste.uiuc.edu/mathed/queryform.html

Mathematics Lessons Database, provided by UIUC's Office for Mathematics, Science, and Technology Education (MSTE), features a database that allows you to search for approximately 50 online, interactive math lessons involving real-life situations for high school students. You can also browse the complete list of the Internet-based math lessons by clicking their titles.

McREL: Lesson Plans and Activities

www.mcrel.org/resources/links/mathlessons.asp

McREL: Lesson Plans and Activities, gathered by Mid-Continent Regional Educational Laboratory (McREL), contains a collection of math lesson plan sites for Grades K–12.

Pi Home Page

www.ncsa.uiuc.edu/edu/RSE/RSEorange/buttons.html

Pi Home Page contains various resources for teaching students in Grades 6–8 all about pi. The site includes lesson plans and activities, facts and history, projects, and applications.

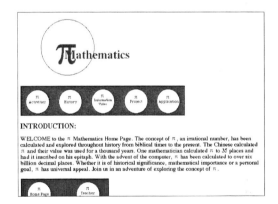

SAMI: Math Resources

www.learner.org/sami/view-category.php3?category=math

Science and Math Initiatives (SAMI), sponsored by the Annenberg Foundation, contains hundreds of math resources for Grades K–12. To find math lesson plans, click List, Search, or Browse.

Scholastic In School

www.scholastic.com/inschool/

Scholastic In School provides a collection of ready-to-use reproducible math activities for Grades 1-6. The worksheets include answer keys and can be used independently of Scholastic materials.

SCORE Mathematics Lessons

http://score.kings.k12.ca.us/lessons.html

The **Schools of California Online Resource for Educators (SCORE)** provides a collection of teacher-developed mathematics lesson plans for Grades K-12 supporting the California Mathematics Standards. Other math plans are included in the yellow panel. All the lessons are organized by topic and by K-7 and 8-12 grade levels.

SMILE Program Mathematics Index

www.iit.edu/~smile/mathinde.html

The **Science and Mathematics Initiative for Learning Enhancement (SMILE)** program, maintained by the Illinois Institute of Technology, features more than 200 math lesson plans developed by teachers for Grades K-12. Topics include arithmetic, geometry and measurement, patterns and logic, probability and statistics, recreational math, practical & applied math, graphs & visuals, and algebra & trigonometry. Each plan includes objectives, the materials needed, suggested strategy, and expected outcomes.

Susan Boone's Lesson Plans

www.crpc.rice.edu/CRPC/GT/sboone/Lessons/lptitle.html

Susan Boone's Lesson Plans provides Internet-based math lessons and activities for Grades 6-12. The activities include interactive projects in which students use math to solve real-life problems related to the Indianapolis 500, census data, real estate trends, and traffic reports.

Suzanne's Mathematics Lessons

http://forum.swarthmore.edu/alejandre/

Suzanne Alejandre provides a wide variety of original Web lessons she created to use with middle school math students. Topics include designs with circles, factoring through geometry, algebraic factoring, tessellations, creating magic squares, polyhedra, and fractals. Other math resources created by the author involve online interactive and classroom technology lessons.

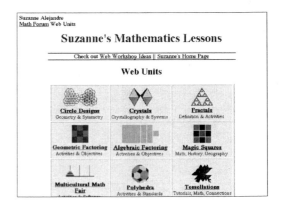

Teachers Helping Teachers

www.pacificnet.net/~mandel/Math.html

Teachers Helping Teachers, updated weekly, is a forum where K-12 teachers can share lesson plans in math and other subject areas. Teachers can also find classroom management ideas and a topic-of-the-week feature by clicking Teachers Helping Teachers Home Page at the bottom of the page.

Teachers.Net Lesson Bank

http://teachers.net/lessons/

The **Teachers.Net Lesson Bank**, a curriculum exchange forum for Grades PK-12, provides a searchable collection of more than 400 lesson plans and activities contributed by teachers. To find math lesson plans, click Mathematics on the left side or Curricula at the top of the page.

TeachersFirst Web Content Matrix

www.teachersfirst.com/matrix-f.htm

TeachersFirst Web Content Matrix, provided by the Network for Instructional Television (NITV), offers a collection of lesson plans at the elementary, middle, and high school levels. To find mathematics plans, scroll to Mathematics in the table, and click lesson plans.

Teaching Ideas for Primary Teachers

www.warner.clara.net/

Teaching Ideas for Primary Teachers, created by Mark Warner, contains a collection of math and time-filler activities to complement a K-5 mathematics curriculum. The site also includes worksheets that can be printed and photocopied for classroom use.

Teaching Mathematics in the Middle and Secondary Schools

http://euclid.barry.edu/~marinas/mat476/lessons.html

Teaching Mathematics in the Middle and Secondary Schools contains 40 lesson plans created by teachers from Florida that require minimum preparation. Most of the lessons are cross-curricular and involve math in practical and real-life situations.

Teachnet.Com

www.teachnet.com/

Teachnet.Com designed by teachers for K-12 teachers, offers mathematics lesson ideas for geometry, maps & graphs, money, real world, terminology, and general areas.

TEAMS Distance Learning: K-12 Lesson Plans

http://teams.lacoe.edu/documentation/places/lessons.html

TEAMS Distance Learning: K-12 Lesson Plans, maintained by the Los Angeles County Office of Education, provides a collection of lessons plan sites for Grades K-12 organized by subject. To find math lesson plans, click Mathematics.

This Is MEGA Mathematics: Los Alamos National Laboratory

www.c3.lanl.gov/mega-math/

This Is MEGA Mathematics: Los Alamos National Laboratory provides seven innovative hands-on math lessons complete with activities and materials for Grades 4-12. Select from among these topics: The Most Colorful Math of All, Games on Graphs, Welcome to the Hotel Infinity, and A Usual Day at Unusual School.

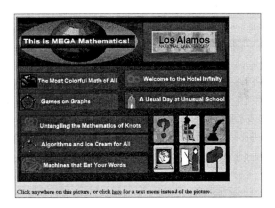

A+ Math

www.aplusmath.com/

A+ Math features an interactive game room where elementary school students can practice online their math skills. Students will find flashcard and advanced problem programs as well as hidden picture and concentration-like games. In addition, students can use a variety of homework tools to check their work.

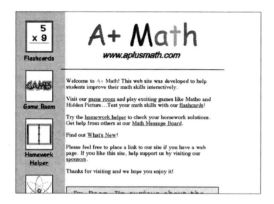

Adam's Puzzles

www.cs.caltech.edu/~adam/PUZZLES/

Adam's Puzzles contains more than 30 puzzles for high school students who have a strong background in calculus and geometry. Detailed answers are provided with a complete explanation.

AIMS Puzzle Corner

www.aimsedu.org/Puzzle/PuzzleList.html

The **AIMS Puzzle Corner**, online since 1995, contains a collection of challenging puzzles for students in Grades K-8. Each puzzle includes a printable worksheet, and the solution for the current month puzzle appears the following month. A new puzzle page is added every month.

Allmath.com

www.allmath.com/

Allmath.com, sponsored by Arbor Media, provides a variety of interactive math resources for elementary school students to practice their basic facts online. It features math flashcards, multiplication tables, a magic square game, and a metric converter. The site also includes biographies of mathematicians and a glossary of math terms.

Ask Dr. Math

http://forum.swarthmore.edu/dr.math/
dr-math.html

The Math Forum's **Ask Dr. Math** provides online math help for Grades K-12. The site is divided into an elementary school, a middle school, and a high school level, and each level includes an archive of hundreds of questions and answers.

Aunt Annie's Crafts: Boxes and Bags

www.auntannie.com/boxbag.html

Aunt Annie's Crafts provides a variety of art projects useful for students learning geometry in Grades 6-12. Students can make their own boxes and bags in different shapes, sizes, and designs. To view these projects on one page, scroll and click all the project selections.

Aunty Math's Fun Math Challenges for Kids

www.dcmrats.org/AuntyMath.html

Aunty Math from DuPage Children's Museum near Chicago posts every two weeks a math challenge for elementary level students, in story form, drawn from her own interactions with her niece and nephews. Students can write in with their answers and get back comments from Aunty Math or others. The site also includes archives of past problems, tip sheets for teachers, as well as extensions to other subjects built into the stories.

Bamdad's Math Comics Page

www.csun.edu/~hcmth014/comics.html

Bamdad's Math Comics Page, frequently updated with new comics, features a collection of more than 200 cartoons scanned from newspapers and magazines. These cartoons, suitable for Grades 5-12, usually involve humorous math-related situations.

BEATCALC: Beat the Calculator!

http://forum.swarthmore.edu/k12/mathtips/ 2digit5.html

The Math Forum provides more than 185 mental calculation shortcuts from B. Lee Clay's **Beat the Calculator (BEATCALC)** mailing list for Grades 5-12. Each shortcut contains a clear explanation and a sample problem. For a list of all the shortcuts, scroll to the bottom of the page and click Full List. The site includes practice problems to accompany these shortcuts. Teachers can subscribe via e-mail to this free weekly service.

Biographies of Women Mathematicians

www.agnesscott.edu/lriddle/women/ women.htm

Biographies of Women Mathematicians is part of an on-going project by students in mathematics classes at Agnes Scott College in Atlanta, Georgia. Included are more than 150 biographies of women mathematicians illustrating their past and present achievements. The site, suitable for Grades 6-12, also offers other math history links.

Brain Teasers

www.eduplace.com/math/brain/

Houghton Mifflin's **Brain Teasers** are provided weekly for students in Grades 3-8. The teasers are organized by grade level, and answers appear the following week. To find archives of brain teasers for Grades 9-12, scroll to the bottom and click McDougal Littell's Spring Brain Teasers Contest.

BU's Interactive WWW Games

http://scv.bu.edu/Games/games.html

Boston University Scientific Computing and Visualization Group provides a collection of online interactive board games students can play on their computers. Games include Pegs, Minesweep, 9 Puzzle, Triple Yahtzee, and WinFive.

Carol Hurst's Math and Children's Literature

www.carolhurst.com/subjects/math/math.html

Carol Hurst's Math and Children's Literature offers a variety of ways to integrate children's literature with math. The site provides ideas and activities from articles Hurst wrote for the *Teaching K–8 Magazine*. It also includes a list of recommended books by grade level and theme.

Clever Games for Clever People

www.cs.uidaho.edu/~casey931/conway/games.html

Clever Games for Clever People, adapted from John Conway's book *On Numbers and Games*, features 17 classroom logic or strategy games for improving the math abilities of middle school and high school students. Each game includes simple rules, a description of the necessary materials, and clear directions for creating the games.

Connect!

www.pomakis.com:81/c4/c4.cgi

Connect! by Keuth Pomakis provides kids in Grades 3–8 with easy-to-follow rules and an attractive game board for playing this popular logic game on the Web. There are two versions of this program; the newer version supports cookies.

CRC Concise Encyclopedia of Mathematics

www.treasure-troves.com/math/math.html

Eric W. Weisstein's **CRC Concise Encyclopedia of Mathematics** is a compendium of mathematical definitions, formulas, figures, tabulations, and references. It is written in an informal style intended to make it accessible to a broad spectrum of readers with a wide range of mathematical backgrounds and interests.

Cyber School Resources

www.accessone.com/~bbunge/

Robert Bunge provides a WorksheetMaker that generates whole number practice worksheets that teachers can print and recopy for use with students in Grades 2–6. In addition, he includes Interactive Algebra exercises, which allow high school students to practice online equations, factoring, and graphing skills. There are multiple levels for each topic and exercise hints.

Dave's Math Tables

www.sisweb.com/math/tables.htm

Dave's Math Tables, available in both English and Spanish versions for Grades 5–12, provides a vast array of math topics from a basic multiplication table to something as mind-boggling as a "fourier series." The site includes an English-Spanish Math Dictionary (link at the bottom of the page).

Desdemona

www.math.hmc.edu/~dmazzoni/
cgi-bin/desmain.cgi

Dominic Mazzoni's **Desdemona** is an interactive Web-based version of the classic game of Othello, also known as Reversi. You play against the computer on a board trying to outflank opponent's discs. The player wins who has the majority of their discs on the board at the end of the game. The site provides rules for how to play the game.

Eight Great Riddles

www.scottforesman.com/sfaw/resources/
riddles/mathrid.html

Scott Foresman Addison Wesley provides eight online math riddles with accompanying answers for students in Grades 3-7.

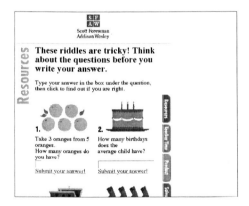

The Family Math Home Page

http://theory.lcs.mit.edu/~emjordan/
famMath.html

The Family Math Home Page, developed by the Lawrence Hall of Science at the University of California, Berkeley, for Grades K-5, provides 10 online math activities from its *Family Math Newsletter*. To find these activities, scroll to Back Issues and click either Issue 1, Issue 2, or Issue 3.

Famous Problems in the History of Mathematics

http://forum.swarthmore.edu/~isaac/
mathhist.html

Isaac Reed presents a collection of some of the great problems that have inspired mathematicians from Zeno to Cantor. Included are problems that are suitable for middle school and high school math students, with links to solutions, as well as links to mathematicians' biographies and other math history sites.

Financial Calculators!

www.hsh.com/calculators.html

Financial Calculators!, maintained by HSH Associates, provides a variety of basic financial calculators that high school students can use to gain a better knowledge of money management strategies.

Finch Math Problems of the Week

www.mbnet.mb.ca/~jfinch/math.html

Mr. Finch offers his collection of weekly math problems for each month of the year. The site includes problems as well as answers for both Grades 3 and 4 and Grades 5 and 6.

Flashcards for Kids

www.edu4kids.com/math/

Infobahn Xpress provides a collection of interactive math flashcards for students in Grades K-8. Students can practice online their basic math computations choosing the skill, the difficulty level, and the numbers to be used. The site also keeps score and informs students when their answers are wrong.

Forum Interactive Projects

http://forum.swarthmore.edu/mathsites/
forum.html

The Math Forum provides a variety of interactive projects featuring online help, problems, and projects for students and teachers in Grades 3-12.

FunBrain.com

www.funbrain.com/

FunBrain.com provides more than 30 online games for students in Grades K-8. Number games include Math Baseball, Change Maker, and Guess the Number. A great feature of the site is the free and easy-to-use Quiz Lab for teachers. Teachers can create their online quizzes for their students, or they can access hundreds of ready-made quizzes prepared by other teachers. The sign-up form is a snap and takes less than a minute!

Fundrum My Conundrum

www.cataloguesonline.com/puzzles/

Fundrum My Conundrum features a collection of 100 riddles, puzzles, and conundrums organized by difficulty level for Grades 4-12. Answers are provided.

Geometry and the Imagination in Minneapolis

www.geom.umn.edu/docs/doyle/mpls/
handouts/handouts.html

Geometry and the Imagination in Minneapolis consists of more than 30 handouts for high school math students. Topics include knots, diagrams and maps, geometry on the sphere, Descartes' formula, topology, Gaussian curvature, and other topics.

The Geometry Center

www.geom.umn.edu/

The Geometry Center, a mathematics research and education center at the University of Minnesota, features a gallery of geometry explorations in Interactive Web Applications and a variety of geometry projects for high school math students in the Course Materials section.

Geometry Junkyard

www.ics.uci.edu/~eppstein/junkyard/

David Eppstein's **Geometry Junkyard** contains a wide variety of attractively illustrated geometry articles for Grades 9-12. Topics include circles and spheres, coloring, covering and packing, dissection, geometric models, and knot theory, as well as the author's own contributions.

Interactive Mathematics Miscellany and Puzzles

www.cut-the-knot.com/

Alexander Bogomolny provides a collection of hundreds of interactive activities and puzzles that illustrate mathematical concepts for high school students and teachers. Topics include games and puzzles, arithmetic, algebra, geometry, probability, proofs, "impossible" math topics, and others. Solutions and explanations are provided for each puzzle.

Interactive Web Games

http://genesis.ne.mediaone.net/games.html

Steve Belczyk provides four interactive Web games for students in Grades 5-12. The games are WebBattleship, WebMinesweeper, WebReversi, and WebMaze.

K-12 Math Problems, Puzzles, Tips & Tricks

http://forum.swarthmore.edu/k12/mathtips/

The Math Forum provides a collection of math problems, puzzles, tips, and tricks for Grades K-12. To find many more sites with math problems and puzzles, click their Library's list.

Lemonade Stand on the Web

www.littlejason.com/lemonade/index.html

Jason Mayans' **Lemonade Stand on the Web** teaches basic business math (sales minus expenses equals profits) to kids in Grades 5-8. The object of the game is to make as much money as possible in 25 rounds. Before each round starts, you review the weather forecast. Then you decide how many cups of lemonade to make, and how much to spend on advertising. At the end of each round, you receive a summary of how many cups sold and how much profit you've made.

The Longevity Game

www.northwesternmutual.com/games/longevity/

The Longevity Game provides a means to calculate how long you can expect to live based on life insurance industry research. Everyone starts with the average life expectancy of 73 years and adds or subtracts years from the score as he or she responds to a questionnaire.

MacTutor History of Mathematics Archive

www-groups.dcs.st-and.ac.uk/~history/

The **MacTutor History of Mathematics Archive**, created by John J. O'Connor and Edmund F. Robertson of the University of St. Andrews in Scotland, features a collection of more than 1,500 biographies of mathematicians, with snapshots arranged in alphabetical and chronological lists. This site, suitable for Grades 6-12, also includes birthplace maps, history topics, an index to female mathematicians, and related Web resources.

Mancala

http://imagiware.com/mancala/

Mancala is an ancient challenging African pit game (a.k.a. Kalaha) involving logic and strategy for Grades 4-12. It includes simple rules to follow and a hint button that helps new players make good moves.

MasterMind

http://itp1.physik.tu-berlin.de/~prengel/MAMI/MasterMind.html

Frank Prengel's **MasterMind** is an online logic game where you try to guess a combination of four colors out of seven in four places that the computer has randomly selected. This interactive game is suitable for students in Grades 5-12.

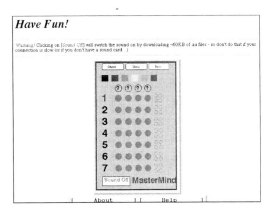

Math and Numbers

http://family.go.com/Categories/Activities/
Features/family_0401_02/dony/donytv_math/
donytv044.html

Math and Numbers, from the online book *365 TV-Free Activities You Can Do With Your Child*, features a collection of math activities for Grades K-6. Among the activities are checker calculator, crazy nines, household Gallup Poll, number hunt, and square five.

Math Archive

http://bsuvc.bsu.edu/~d004ucslabs/

Kirill Safarov provides a collection of more than 200 math problems, ranging from common sense problems to algebra and calculus, for Grades 5-12. Most of the problems include solutions.

Math Education and Technology

www.ies.co.jp/math/indexeng.html

The Japanese company, International Education Software (IES), provides online an amazing Manipula Math collection of nearly 200 interactive, animated Java applet programs that dynamically illustrate mathematical concepts for middle and high school students. The site, updated bimonthly, includes applets for geometry, trigonometry, calculus, and for miscellaneous math topics.

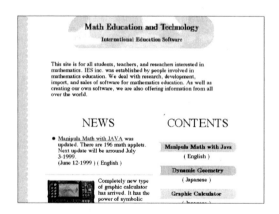

The Math Forum

http://forum.swarthmore.edu/

The Math Forum, sponsored by Swarthmore College, is a one-stop Internet guide for all your K-12 math needs. It features lesson plans, interactive activities, materials, and Web sites related to teaching arithmetic, algebra, geometry, and advanced math topics.

Math Parent Handbook

www.eduplace.com/math/res/parentbk/

Houghton Mifflin's **Math Parent Handbook** provides a collection of refrigerator math puzzles (with solutions) and 13 quick-and-easy math games that can motivate elementary school kids to like math.

Math Pages

www.seanet.com/~ksbrown/

Kevin Brown's **Math Pages** is a treasure chest of information containing more than 300 articles on a variety of mathematical topics for teachers of advanced level math courses. Topics include number theory, combinatorics, geometry, algebra, calculus, differential equations, probability, statistics, physics, and the history of math.

MathStories.com

www.mathstories.com/

MathStories.com, updated regularly, contains a wide variety of ready-to-use worksheets with more than 1,000 word problems for Grades 1-5. The problems are classified by grade and topic. Topics include whole number operations, fractions, and decimals. In addition, there's a Magic with Numbers section with interesting number puzzle worksheets.

Math Tutor

www.urawa.cabletv.ne.jp/users/pm3/math/index.html

Math Tutor provides online math assistance for a wide variety of topics, including addition, multiplication, decimals, fractions, factorization, and more. You use an online calculator, and it keeps a record of your performance. The site is suitable for Grades 2-12.

Math Work

www.coastlink.com/users/sbryce/mathwork/

Scott Bryce's **Math Work** allows elementary school teachers to create and print math worksheets for addition, subtraction, multiplication, and division of whole numbers.

Monster Math

www.lifelong.com/lifelong_universe/AcademicWorld/MonsterMath/NTEng/NTHowToPlay.html

Lifelong's **Monster Math**, available in English, Spanish, and Italian, is an online interactive, story for the primary grades. The site is designed to introduce and review a variety of basic math concepts, such as counting, addition, and multiplication, and kids answer simple number questions about a monster to advance in the story.

Mrs. Glosser's Math Goodies: Interactive Lesson Plans

www.mathgoodies.com/lessons/

Mrs. Glosser provides an online collection of 32 interactive lessons in geometry, percent, number theory, and integers for middle school students. The site includes an answer for each exercise along with a detailed explanation.

National Council of Teachers of Mathematics

www.nctm.org/

The **National Council of Teachers of Mathematics (NCTM)** is the largest professional organization for improving the teaching of mathematics at the K-12 grade levels. Click Publications to find classroom activities from *Teaching Children Mathematics*, *Mathematics Teaching in the Middle School*, and *The Mathematics Teacher*.

Panthera's Puzzle Contest

www.puzzleu.com/pow/

Panthera's Puzzle Contest enables kids in Grades 4-8 to e-mail their solutions to 42 puzzles. It also includes the solutions to the previous 42 puzzles. To play grid-type logic games online, click Light Puzzles.

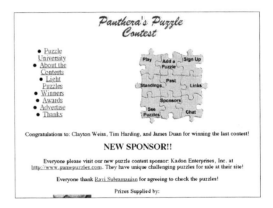

The Pi-Search Page

www.aros.net/~angio/pi_stuff/piquery.html

The Pi-Search Page, suitable for Grades 8-12, helps students unravel the mystery of irrational numbers. Students can enter any number and determine its location in pi. For example, by choosing July 4, 1776, and entering 070476, students can find out where that set of numbers is in pi's unending sequence of digits.

The Prime Pages

www.utm.edu/research/primes/

The Prime Pages offers a vast collection of material about prime numbers, including the sieve of Erastothenes, lists of prime numbers and factorizations, the Mersenne primes, and a general historical introduction to primes. The site is suitable for Grades 8-12.

Problem of the Day

www.highland.madison.k12.il.us/jbasden/
problems/

Jon Basden provides a collection of 170 math problems he used with his middle school students during the 1998–99 school year. To find the other problems, scroll to the bottom of the page. For another 175 problems from the previous school year, type the following URL in your browser: www.highland.madison.k12.il.us/jbasden/oldmath/97_98_pods.html

Problem of the Week Home Page

www.wits.ac.za/ssproule/pow.htm

Stephen Sproule provides a collection of problem-of-the-week sites organized by grade level for Grades K-12.

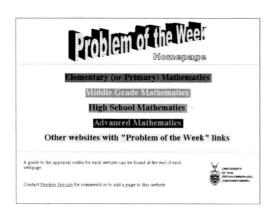

The rec.puzzles Archive

http://einstein.et.tudelft.nl/~arlet/puzzles/

The rec.puzzles Archive, maintained by Arlet Ottens, contains tons of puzzles and brain teasers categorized by topic for Grades 9-12. The puzzles were compiled from various sources, and each puzzle includes a solution.

RHL School

www.rhlschool.com/

RHL School provides weekly printable worksheets to complement any math program in Grades 4-8. It includes a collection of worksheets for computation and problem solving. Teachers can request a free weekly updated answer key sent by e-mail.

Saxon Online Math Activities

www.saxonpub.com/tech/online_activities.html

Saxon Publishers provides a variety of online math games and problems for Grades K-12. The site includes interactive basic facts and multiple counting practice, a kindergarten pattern block game, and math enrichment and math stumper problems.

Shack's Math Problems

www.thewizardofodds.com/math/

Shack's Math Problems contains a collection of more than 135 math and logic problems ranging from basic math to differential equations. Each problem includes a difficulty rating, an answer, and usually a solution with an explanation. The site is suitable for Grades 7-12.

S.O.S. MATHematics

www.math.utep.edu/sosmath/

S.O.S. MATHematics from the University of Texas at El Paso contains a wide variety of online worksheets for algebra, trigonometry, calculus, and other advanced math topics for students in Grades 7-12. Each exercise includes a set of problems and answers giving clear explanations and appropriate practice so that students can check their understanding and monitor their progress.

The Sphinx

http://stud1.tuwien.ac.at/~e9226344/Themes/Puzzles/sphinx.html

The Sphinx offers a variety of math and logic puzzles sorted by category and level of difficulty for Grades 8-12. Some solutions are provided.

Sprott's Fractal Gallery

http://sprott.physics.wisc.edu/fractals.htm

Sprott's Fractal Gallery is suitable for Grades 6-12. Every day, it presents a new fractal that is automatically generated by the author, Julien C. Sprott. The site contains an archive of previous fractals and links to thousands of fractal patterns from other sources.

Teacher2Teacher

http://forum.swarthmore.edu/t2t/

The Math Forum's **Teacher2Teacher** is an online resource for K-12 teachers who have questions about teaching math. This service provides an archive of answers, pages of public discussions, and a form for submitting questions.

21st Century Problem Solving

www.hawaii.edu/suremath/home1.html

Howard McAllister's **21st Century Problem Solving** features the author's instructional approach to problem solving that applies across the curriculum and at all grade levels. The site provides numerous examples of problems solved using the author's problem solving methods, a discussion of the principles of reliable problem solving, and an evolving encyclopedia of solved problems in pre-college algebra, physics, and chemistry. For a list of all the solved problems, click Solved.

The Universal Currency Converter

www.xe.net/currency/

The Universal Currency Converter includes simple instructions that allow middle school students to perform interactive foreign-exchange-rate conversions on the Internet.

WebMath

www.webmath.com/

WebMath provides instant solutions to hundreds of math problems for students in Grades 3-12. It generates immediate answers to their specific math questions from the problems that they enter. The site also shows them how to arrive at an answer and provides a step-by-step solution. Students can find answers to a wide variety of math problems for everyday math, units conversion, graphing, polynomials, quadratic equations, word problems, computational problems, finding factors, GCFs, and LCMs, addition to division fraction problems, simplifying expressions, and even calculus derivative problems.

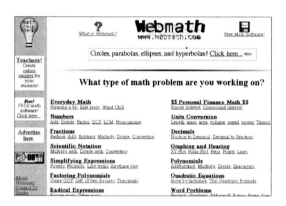

Word Problems for Kids

www.stfx.ca/special/mathproblems/

Word Problems for Kids, from St. Francis Xavier University in Canada, is designed for Grades 5-12 to help students improve their problem-solving skills. The problems are classified by grade levels, and each problem includes a hint and an answer.

Worksheet Generator

www.caverns.com/~mkt/Mathematics/worksheetGenerator.html

Michael Thompson's **Worksheet Generator** creates online printable math worksheets for Grades 4-9. Each worksheet can have up to 50 problems with a variety of whole number, integer, equation, greatest common factor, least common multiple, or algebra problems. Each worksheet includes a heading, a page layout, and an accompanying answer key.

Zini's Activity Pages

www.incwell.com/Zini/

Zini's Activity Pages provides a collection of 35 printable, fun math activity pages for early childhood education.

Multicultural

About.com Multiculturalism Guide Site

http://home.about.com/culture/cultureamer/

About.com Multiculturalism Guide Site is created by a qualified About.com Guide, a subject specialist in multiculturalism, who's responsible for helping you get the most out of your time online. It contains netlinks, articles, forums, a chat room, a multiculturalism newsletter, and a search engine.

The Awesome Library Multicultural Lesson Plans

www.neat-schoolhouse.org/Library/
Materials_Search/Lesson_Plans/
Multicultural.html

The Awesome Library Multicultural Lesson Plans offers teachers in K–12 more than 30 lesson plans with a multicultural theme.

The Awesome Library Multicultural Resources

www.awesomelibrary.org/Classroom/
Social_Studies/Multicultural/Multicultural.html

The Awesome Library Multicultural Resources provides links to more than 60 subtopics. The site also includes discussions, lesson plans, lists, materials, papers, periodicals, projects, and purchase resources.

Hall of Multiculturalism

www.tenet.edu/academia/multi.html

Hall of Multiculturalism provides a list of multicultural resources for K–12 teachers and students. It includes links to African and African-American Resources, Asian and Asian-American Resources, Cross-Category Multicultural Resources, Indigenous People Resources, Latino/Chicano/Hispano/Mexican Resources, and Native American Resources.

Intercultural E-Mail Classroom Connections

www.stolaf.edu/network/iecc/

Intercultural E-Mail Classroom Connections includes mailing lists provided by St. Olaf College as a free service to help teachers and classes link with partners in other countries and cultures for e-mail classroom pen pal and project exchanges.

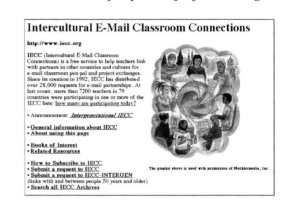

Making Multicultural Connections Through Trade Books Lesson Index

www.mcps.k12.md.us/curriculum/socialstd/
MBD/Lessons_index.html

Making Multicultural Connections Through Trade Books Lesson Index, from the Montgomery (Maryland) County Public Schools, features multicultural trade books for elementary school students. In some instances specific lessons are included to illustrate how the trade book can be used as a classroom activity. Bibliographical information and a very brief synopsis are also provided for each book.

Multicultural Calendar

www.kidlink.org/KIDPROJ/MCC/

Multicultural Calendar, part of the KIDLINK Project, allows students to browse by month, author, country, or holiday. The entries contain recipes for holiday foods, historical background, significance of the holidays, and the special ways in which these days are observed.

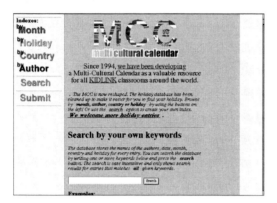

Multicultural Pavilion

http://curry.edschool.Virginia.EDU:80/go/multicultural/home.html

Multicultural Pavilion, sponsored by the University of Virginia and created by Paul Gorski, provides materials for teachers interested in multicultural issues. Click Teacher's Corner to find resources for K-12 teachers, including reviews of children's music, multicultural activities, online archives, and links to multicultural Web sites.

Multisubjects

The Academy Curriculum Exchange

http://ofcn.org/cyber.serv/academy/ace/

The Academy Curriculum Exchange offers hundreds of K-12 minilesson plans for math, science, social studies, language arts, and other subjects.

Apple Learning Exchange
Lesson Plans Library

http://henson.austin.apple.com/edres/
lessonmenu.shtml

Apple Learning Exchange provides a collection of technology lesson plans written by teachers and organized by grade level and topics for Grades K-12. Topics include art, cross-curricular, language arts, mathematics, science, social studies, and general.

Ask Jeeves

www.askjeeves.com/

Ask Jeeves a question in plain English and this Internet butler will retrieve the information you've requested instantly. For example, type "Where can I find K-12 lesson plans?" and he'll find answers for you using popular search engines.

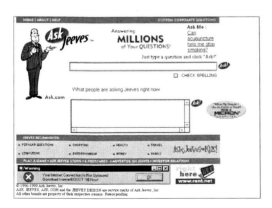

AskERIC Lesson Plans

http://ericir.syr.edu/Virtual/Lessons/

The **AskERIC** collection contains more than 1,000 lesson plans contributed by teachers from all over the United States. They cover all grade levels and subject areas.

Awesome Library: Lesson Plans

www.awesomelibrary.org/Library/
Materials_Search/Lesson_Plans/
Lesson_Plans.html

Awesome Library organizes your exploration of the World Wide Web with 10,000 carefully reviewed resources for all K-12 curriculum areas including a lesson plan directory.

Baltimore Curriculum Project
Lesson Plans

www.cstone.net/~bcp/BCPIntro2.htm

Baltimore Curriculum Project Lesson Plans, based on the Core Knowledge Sequence, features monthly K-5 lesson plans for a variety of curricular areas. The lesson plans, organized by grade level and subject, are presented in a table.

Big Sky Gopher Menu

gopher://bvsd.k12.co.us:70/11/
Educational_Resources/Lesson_Plans/
Big%20Sky/

Big Sky Gopher Menu features a collection of K-12 lesson plans for a variety of curriculum areas.

Blue Web'n Learning Applications

www.kn.pacbell.com/wired/bluewebn/

Blue Web'n Learning Applications, provided by Pacific Bell, includes lessons, activities, projects, resources, references, and tools for the K-12 teacher. Scroll to Content Table to find more than 150 lesson plans for various subject areas.

CEC Lesson Plans

www.col-ed.org/cur/

CEC Lesson Plans, sponsored by the Columbia Education Center in Portland, Oregon, features a wide variety of lesson plans created by teachers for use in their own classrooms.

Educast Lesson Plan Search

www.educast.com/arc/lp/lessonPlanSrch.html

Educast Lesson Plan Search, designed by Davidson and Associates for Grades K-12, provides a collection of more than 525 lesson plans that is updated weekly. Each lesson plan includes printable student activity sheets that require Adobe's free Acrobat Reader.

Educate the Children: Lesson Plans and Worksheet Resources

www.educate.org.uk/lessons.htm

Educate the Children provides elementary school teachers with hundreds of educational lesson plans and worksheets for many subject areas. Each lesson includes a title, a description, and an ability level. To view or print these materials, Adobe's free Acrobat Reader has to be installed on your computer.

Education World: Lesson Planning Center

www.education-world.com/a_lesson/

Education World: Lesson Planning Center, sponsored by American Fidelity for Grades K-12, provides a weekly article focusing on a specific topical theme, such as hurricanes, first day of school, whales, or a specific holiday. In each article, teachers will find cross-curriculum lessons and activities related to the arts, history, language arts, math, science, social studies, and other topics. Each article offers printable student worksheets and links to relevant sites. In addition, scroll and click Lesson Planning Resources in the SECTION GUIDE to find hundreds of other lesson plan sources.

Encarta Lesson Collection

www.encarta.msn.com/schoolhouse/

Encarta Lesson Collection offers a collection of hundreds of lesson plans contributed by K-12 teachers in a wide variety of subject areas.

Gryphon House, Inc.

www.ghbooks.com/

Gryphon House, Inc., a leading publisher of children's activity books for ages 2-7, provides hundreds of cross-curricular activities taken directly from more than 40 of the company's books. Click Free Activities to find all this material.

Helping Your Child Series

www.ed.gov/pubs/parents/hyc.html

U.S. Department of Education provides the **Helping Your Child Series** containing more than 150 fun activities for Grades K-8. Included are writing, geography, history, math, and science activities. Selected titles are written in Spanish.

Houghton Mifflin Activity Search

www.eduplace.com/search/activity2.html

Houghton Mifflin Activity Search features a database for finding K-8 lesson plans in language arts, math, social studies, science, and art. Activities can also be browsed by theme.

Index to Internet Lesson Plan Sites for K-12 Educators

http://falcon.jmu.edu/~ramseyil/lesson.htm

The Internet School Library Media Center at James Madison University provides an immense collection of lesson plan sites collected by Inez Ramsey and indexed by major subject areas. The list also includes general (multisubject) lesson plan sites.

Kathy Schrock's Guide for Educators: Lesson Plans and Thinking Skills

http://discoveryschool.com/schrockguide/edles.html

Kathy Schrock's Guide for Educators features a selective collection of lesson plan sites for Grades K-12.

PBS TeacherSource

www.pbs.org/teachersource/

PBS TeacherSource features an inventory of more than 1,000 free lesson plans, teacher guides, and online activities that complement PBS television programs. Using the keyword feature Find It!, teachers can find lesson plans for a variety of topics for Grades 4-12. Many of these plans can be used independently of the TV programs.

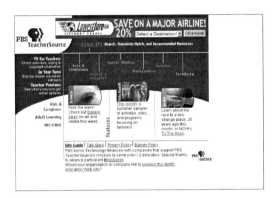

Project Center

www.eduplace.com/projects/

Project Center, from Houghton Mifflin, features a variety of Internet-based cooperative projects in reading, math, social studies, science, and other areas for K-12 classrooms. Teachers can also post their own projects by e-mail, and new projects are added weekly.

ProTeacher

www.proteacher.com/020002.shtml

ProTeacher, a resource for K-12 teachers, provides a collection of lesson plan sites for language arts, science, social studies, math, and physical education. The site also includes online activities and lessons for language arts, math, and science.

Richard's Education Page

www.edu.yorku.ca/~tcs/~rfouchaux/
edu_urls.htm

Richard's Education Page contains a variety of
lesson plans in language arts, math, science, and
social studies for Grades K-12. To find these
plans, click LSNPLNS in the top menu bar.

Ron MacKinnon's Educational Bookmarks

http://juliet.stfx.ca/people/stu/x94emj/
bookmark.html

Ron MacKinnon's Educational Bookmarks
provides a vast collection of sites for K-12 lesson
plans in math, science, social studies, foreign
languages, and other curriculum areas.

Stephanie's Lesson Plans

http://users.twave.net/sashley/lesson.htm

Stephanie's Lesson Plans is a list of K-12 lesson
plans for language arts, social studies, science,
math, computer skills, art, and miscellaneous
areas.

Teachers Helping Teachers

http://pacificnet.net/~mandel/

Teachers Helping Teachers is a source for lesson
plans and suggestions contributed by teachers.
The site includes plans for classroom
management, language arts, science, social
studies, the arts, and special education.

Teachers.Net Lesson Bank

http://teachers.net/lessons/

The **Teachers.Net Lesson Bank**, a curriculum
exchange forum for Grades PK-12, provides a
searchable collection of more than 400 lesson
plans and activities contributed by teachers.

TeachersFirst Web Content Matrix

www.teachersfirst.com/matrix-f.htm

TeachersFirst Web Content Matrix, provided by
the Network for Instructional Television (NITV),
offers a collection of hundreds of lesson plans at
the elementary, middle, and high school level. To
find plans for a variety of subjects, click lesson
plans for the desired subject in the table.

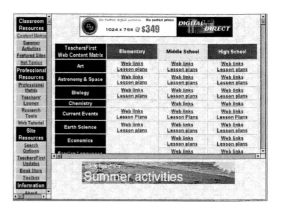

Teachnet.Com: Lesson Ideas

www.teachnet.com/

Teachnet.Com designed by teachers for K-12
teachers, offers lesson ideas for many subjects,
including Language Arts, Math, Science, Social
Studies, and Miscellaneous areas.

Music

ARTSEDGE Instructional Resources for Teaching the Performing Arts

http://artsedge.kennedy-center.org/cs/perfarts.html

The Kennedy Center's **ARTSEDGE Instructional Resources for Teaching the Performing Arts** contains online curriculum units, lessons and activities for teaching music in Grades K-12.

AskERIC Lesson Plans: Music

http://ericir.syr.edu/Virtual/Lessons/Arts/Music/

AskERIC Lesson Plans: Music provides a collection of a short list of music lesson plans contributed by teachers for Grades K-12.

EGMT&L Center

www2.potsdam.edu/crane/campbemr/lessons/

Elementary General Music Teaching and Learning Center contains a collection of music lesson plans for Grades K-6.

Encarta Lesson Collection

www.encarta.msn.com/schoolhouse/lessons/

Encarta Lesson Collection offers a collection of lesson plans contributed by K-12 teachers in various subject areas. To find music education plans, select Arts and then click Music.

Fine Arts K to 7

www.bced.gov.bc.ca/irp/fak7/fak7toc.htm

Fine Arts K to 7, provided by British Columbia's Ministry of Education, includes an integrated package of lesson plans for teaching music in Grades K-7. Scroll to Music K to 7 Curriculum to find the plans.

GEM: Subject Arts—Music Pre-K to 12

www.thegateway.org/index2/artsmusic.html

The **Gateway to Educational Materials (GEM)**, sponsored by the U.S. Department of Education, provides a collection of art and music lesson plans and instructional resources for Grades PK-12.

The Lesson Plans Page

www.lessonplanspage.com/index.htm

The Lesson Plans Page, by Kyle Yamnitz, contains a collection of music lesson plans for Grades K-6.

Music Education Launch Site

www.talentz.com/

Music Education Launch Site, created by Jeff Brenan for Grades K-12, provides a collection of music education lesson plans organized by school level and topic.

Music 8 to 10

www.bced.gov.bc.ca/irp/music810/mutoc.htm

Music 8 to 10, provided by British Columbia's Ministry of Education, features an integrated package of lesson plans for teaching music in Grades 8, 9, and 10.

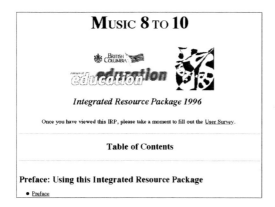

Music Teacher Resources

http://home.earthlink.net/~bluesman1/teacher.html

Music Teacher Resources contains a variety of lesson plans for Grades 4–12, including African and Native American plans.

The Blue Flame Cafe

www.blueflamecafe.com/

The Blue Flame Cafe contains an interactive biographical encyclopedia of the great blues singers from Muddy Waters to Stevie Ray Vaughan with photos and music clips. The site is suitable for Grades 7-12.

Charles K. Moss Piano Studio

http://classicalmus.interspeed.net/

Charles K. Moss Piano Studio provides a collection of hundreds of links to classical music sites for Grades 8-12.

Children's Music Web Guide

http://cmw.cowboy.net/WebG/

The **Children's Music Web Guide**, created by Monty Harper, contains a searchable and browsable database of hundreds of children's music sites for Grades K-12. Categories include Elementary Education, Fun, Live Music, Media, Music Education, Musicians/Bands, Resources, and songs.

Children's Music Web's Radio Refrigerator

www.childrensmusic.org/fridge.html

The **Children's Music Web's Radio Refrigerator** features a collection of fun children's songs that you can listen to on your computer through RealAudio. The site is suitable for preschool to sixth grade.

Classical Composers' Archive

http://spight.physics.unlv.edu/picgalr2.html

Classical Composers' Archive contains a picture gallery of more than 300 composers, along with biographical information, for Grades 7-12. Each day a new picture of a birthday composer is featured.

Classical Composers Database

http://utopia.knoware.nl/users/jsmeets/

Classical Composers Database, prepared by Jos Smeets, provides information on more than 1,000 composers for Grades 7-12.

The Classical MIDI Archives

www.prs.net/midi.html

The Classical MIDI Archives, arranged in alphabetical order, offers thousands of classical music clips you can listen to at the click of the mouse. Select the Classical MIDI Archives banner and then click the desired composer's initial files. Most composers are represented. You can also use the Control Panel's keyword search engine to find a piece of classical music. The site, suitable for Grades 7-12, also offers a chronology of selected composers in a timeline as well as biographies on more than 125 composers.

The Classical MIDI Connection

http://midiworld.com/cmc/

The Classical MIDI Connection provides thousands of classical music clips organized in libraries, from Renaissance to 20th-century composers for the music enthusiast. The site, suitable for high school, includes MIDI tutorials.

Classical Music

www.serve.com/Reid/legit.htm

Classical Music, a well-organized resource for students in Grades 5-12, is a good starting point for information on classical music. The site, arranged by periods, includes a chart that lists the dates, composers, and timelines in which they wrote, as well as sound clips of famous pieces of music for your listening pleasure.

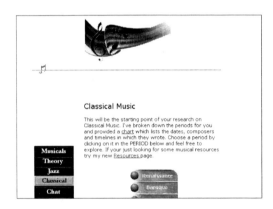

The Classical Music Pages

http://w3.rz-berlin.mpg.de/cmp/classmus.html

The Classical Music Pages, created by Matt Boynick, provides a searchable database of almost everything you need concerning classical music. The site includes history, biographical information about composers (with portraits and short sound examples), explanations of the various musical forms, and a dictionary of musical terms. It is useful to everyone from beginners to the music professional.

ClassicalNet Home Page

www.classical.net/

ClassicalNet Home Page, for Grades 5-12, provides a wide array of resources about classical music. The site includes a list of recommended CDs, biographical data about famous composers, and more than 2,500 related links.

Fun Music Ideas

www.funmusicideas.com/

Fun Music Ideas is a free monthly e-mail newsletter that is electronically mailed to subscribers once a month. It is jam-packed with helpful ideas, songs, games, teaching techniques, and is a virtual tool kit for anyone involved in teaching music. To view online past issues dating back to 1997, scroll to Index by Issue.

Index of Rounds

www-personal.umich.edu/~msmiller/rounds.html

Index of Rounds contains a collection of rounds, including images of the music, lyrics, and sound clips for Grades 4-12.

Internet Music Resource Guide

www.teleport.com/~celinec/music.shtml

Internet Music Resource Guide features links to a variety of music resources, including bands and artists, magazines, and search sites. For an extensive list of everything musical on the Web, click General Sites.

Internet Resources for Music Teachers

www.isd77.k12.mn.us/resources/staffpages/
shirk/music.html

Cynthia M. Shirk has collected **Internet Resources for Music Teachers**, including K-12 Resources for Music Educators, with many links from band leaders to vocal teachers.

Jack Will

http://home.ican.net/~jackw/top.htm

Jack Will offers a collection of some of the songwriter's fun sing-along music for elementary school kids. To play a song on the computer, click midi file; to view its lyrics, click the picture right above the midi file; and to print the song, use your browser's print button.

Jazz MIDI Homepage

www.geocities.com/BourbonStreet/Quarter/
2732/

Petar Bugarchich's **Jazz MIDI Homepage** contains a collection of the jazz MIDI sequences for Grades 5-12. Listening categories include Latin Beat, Medium Groove, Swing, Blues, and the featured artist, Antonio Carlos Jobim. The site also includes links to an assortment of jazz resources.

Jazz Online

www.jazzonln.com/

Jazz Online contains reviews, artist bios, music and video clips, events and club listings, radio links, and more.

John Phillip Sousa Page

www.dws.org/sousa/

John Phillip Sousa Page contains hundreds of sound clips of this great American composer's band music that you can listen to on your computer. The site, suitable for Grades 3-12, also includes related links, photos, and historical information on the March King's life.

Judy and David Page

http://judyanddavid.com/

The **Judy and David Page** is the site for the Canadian music show for preschool and elementary school kids. Teachers will find a catalog of children's music, which includes the lyrics to many popular children's songs. Photos from the show, sound clips of some of the show's music, and links to other children's sites are also featured.

Land of Music

www.landofmusic.com/

The **Land of Music** provides songs and activities to teach the theory concept in the primary grades. It's the home of the Note Family, the Rest Family, and many more characters, making notes, other musical symbols, and instruments come alive for the kids. Everyone in the Land of Music helps to build Songhouses (songs) of all styles. They teach how to read, write, and enjoy music through songs, stories, games, movement, puzzles, and books.

Looney Tunes Karaoke

www.kids.warnerbros.com/karaoke/

Looney Tunes Karaoke, from Warner Brothers, contains 10 popular songs that kids in Grades K-3 can sing, hear, and read.

Mama Lisa's World

www.mamalisa.com/world/

Mama Lisa's World contains a collection of children's songs and nursery rhymes from all over the globe, in English and their native languages. The site is suitable for Grades K-6.

Mark Corey's Music Stuff!

www.mcs.net/~mcorey/mustuf.htm

Mark Corey's Music Stuff! contains a collection of Web sites for band, orchestra, and choir directors, as well as musicians and music educators. The site is suitable for Grades K-12.

MIDI's for Kiddies

www.concentric.net/~Gamba/

MIDI's for Kiddies contains a collection of children's music written by D.F. Saphra for Grades 4-8. Categories include African American history songs, seasonal songs, and health and safety songs. You can listen to the music on your computer as well as print many of the lyrics for use in the classroom.

MoJo's Musical Mouseum

www.kididdles.com/mouseum/

MoJo's Musical Mouseum, created by KIDiddles for Grades K-5, contains a collection of more than the 250 lyrics to children's songs, organized alphabetically and by subject. You can also use a keyword search engine to find a song, as well as request that your favorite song to be listed on the site.

Music Education for Young Children

www.2-life.com/meyc/

Music Education for Young Children, maintained by Deborah Pratt, features teaching ideas, songs and music games, music curricula, and other resources for Grades PK-12.

Music Education Online

www.geocities.com/Athens/2405/

Music Education Online, maintained by Larry Newman, features an interactive message board and chat room, hundreds of links, news articles, and book reviews for Grades K-12.

Music Education Resources

www.bright.net/~lruggles/musiced.html

Music Education Resources catalogs hundreds of links dealing with Music Theory, Music Software, Lyrics, Music History, Resources, Professional Organizations, FTP Sites, Music Clip Art, and Instrumental Sites for Grades K-12.

Music Games Page

http://home.earthlink.net/~bluesman1/games.html

The **Music Games Page** provides ideas and classroom activities for making learning music fun in Grades 4-8. For additional ideas, be sure to click on What's New? More Games!

Music History 102: A Guide to Western Composers and Their Music

www.ipl.org/exhibit/mushist/

Internet Public Library's **Music History 102** is a survey of western classical music from the middle ages to the 20th century for high school students. The guide includes information on more than 30 composers, music clips, and images of each historical period.

Music Lyrics

http://home.earthlink.net/~jmak/Music/Lyrics.html

Music Lyrics, collected by Sue Wichers for Grades K-12, is a list of links to many lyrics sites, including folk, international, scouts, kids, by artists, and others. Some of the sites include sound clips.

Music Notes Interactive

http://hyperion.advanced.org/15413/index.htm

Music Notes Interactive lets you explore online various styles of music from Bach to rock. The site provides information on note reading, intervals, scales, chords, and other useful music education topics for Grades 7-12.

Music Teacher's Resource Site

www.bobchilds.co.uk/mtrs/

The **Music Teacher's Resource Site** includes an Ask-an-expert page where you can find online help from a list of music education experts, equipment and instrument reviews, arrangements and class projects, vocal and instrumental rounds, as well as lyrics you can print out and songs with MIDI files you can enjoy listening to on your computer.

MusicStaff.Com: Music Teaching Articles

www.musicstaff.com/lounge/ideas.htm

MusicStaff.Com provides a collection of articles containing teaching ideas for K-12 music educators. To find a wonderful collection of music sites, click Music Links under teacher services.

OperaGlass

http://rick.stanford.edu/opera/main.html

OperaGlass provides a variety of opera resources for Grades 9-12. The site includes 100 well-known and lesser-known opera composers, with complete opera lists and links to pages containing information on about 250 operas with synopses, libretti, performance histories, discographies, and essays.

Phil's Famous Movie and TV Music Themes

http://freespace.virgin.net/philip.churchyard/pc4.html

Phil's Famous Movie and TV Music Themes is a collection of sound clips from scores of popular movie and TV shows you can listen to on your computer. The site is suitable for Grades K-12.

The Piano Education Page

www.unm.edu/~loritaf/pnoedmn.html

The Piano Education Page, in English and Spanish, contains tips on learning to play the piano, a competition calendar, finding the right piano teacher, getting information on music software, more than 600 music-related sites, and other music education resources for Grades K-12. The site also includes an audition room that offers 500 piano music and sound clips for your listening pleasure with links to composer biographies. Kids can visit Just for Kids to play games and meet composers.

Pure Illusion MIDI Collection

www.facethemusic.org/midisite/

Pure Illusion MIDI Collection contains an eclectic collection of music that students in Grades 6-12 can enjoy listening to on the computer. The site includes fun classical, rock'n'roll, television themes, the movies, Disney, kids, oldies, soul, and motown.

Robert's Midi Jukebox

http://meltingpot.fortunecity.com/kentish/116/midi/

Robert's Midi Jukebox features a list of more than 300 sound clips from the movies, TV programs, and pop songs for your listening pleasure. The site is suitable for Grades 4-12.

Schoolhouse Rock

http://genxtvland.simplenet.com/SchoolHouseRock/index-lo.shtml

Schoolhouse Rock lets you take a trip back to the 1970s. The site contains more than 40 original Schoolhouse Rock songs for different subject areas to share with students in Grades 3-6.

This Day In Music History

http://DataDragon.com/day/

This Day In Music History presents daily the birthdays of well-known composers and songwriters, the openings of Broadway shows and plays, and links to songs that made the charts. The site is suitable for Grades 7-12.

Yahoo!: Classical Composers

www.yahoo.com/Entertainment/Music/Genres/
Classical/Composers/

Yahoo!: Classical Composers introduces students in Grades 5-12 to hundreds of composers from the baroque to the 20th-century periods. Select a musical period and click a composer's name to find biographical information, pictures, and descriptions of the composer's work.

Yahoo!: Genres

http://dir.yahoo.com/Entertainment/Music/
Genres/

Yahoo!: Genres contains a collection of hundreds of sites to every kind of musical style, including children's, classical, folk, jazz, rock, and pop for Grades K-12.

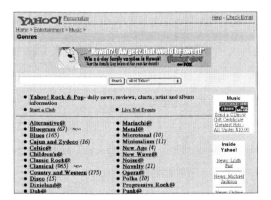

Science

The Academy Curriculum Exchange

http://ofcn.org/cyber.serv/academy/ace/

The Academy Curriculum Exchange offers lesson plans for Grades K-12 in a variety of subject areas. To find more than 200 plans for science, click Elementary School, Intermediate School, or High School.

Access Excellence Activities Exchange

www.accessexcellence.org/AE/

Access Excellence Activities Exchange, sponsored by Genentech, contains an archive of hundreds of lessons and activities submitted by high school biology and life sciences teachers participating in the Access Excellence Program.

ACCESS INDIANA Teaching & Learning Center

http://tlc.ai.org/

The **ACCESS INDIANA Teaching & Learning Center** provides a collection of science lesson plans for Grades K-12. To find them, click Teacher Lesson Plans in the Science section.

Activity Search

www.eduplace.com/search/activity2.html

Activity Search, from Houghton Mifflin, features a curriculum database in which K-8 teachers can search for science lesson plans/activities and other subject areas by grade level. Activities can also be browsed by theme.

Africanized Honey Bees on the Move Lesson Plans

http://ag.arizona.edu/pubs/insects/ahb/

Africanized Honey Bees on the Move Lesson Plans, maintained by Roberta Gibson at the University of Arizona, features 30 lesson plans for Grades K-12 organized by grade clusters. The plans are also integrated with information and activity sheets.

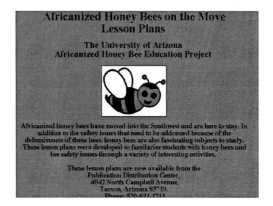

Air Quality Lesson Plans and Data

www.tnrcc.state.tx.us/air/monops/lessons/lesson_plans.html

Air Quality Lesson Plans and Data, provided by the Texas Natural Resource Conservation Commission, features a collection of lesson plans and activities to teach the subject of air quality in the K-12 classroom.

ALCOMed

http://olbers.kent.edu/alcomed/Sam_Net/samnet.html

Advanced Liquid Crystalline Optical Materials (ALCOM) Education Outreach Program provides a collection of K-12 lesson plans prepared by a team of teachers participating in two workshops at Kent State University. Links to the plans can be found at the bottom of the page.

Amazing Science at the Roxy

www.hood-consulting.com/amazing/
qt_amazing/asr.html

Amazing Science at the Roxy, provided by Hood Consulting Group, features a collection of physical science lesson plans and experiments for Grades 5-12.

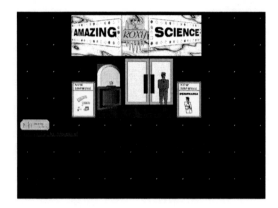

Amazing Space

http://amazing-space.stsci.edu/

The Space Telescope Science Institute, responsible for the scientific operation of the Hubble Space Telescope, provides a variety of interactive Web-based space lessons and activities for Grades 6-12. All lessons include spectacular photographs taken by the Hubble Space Telescope. Activities offered are Galaxies Galore, Star Light, Star Bright, Solar System Trading Cards, Hubble Deep Field Academy, Astronaut Challenge, and Galileo to the Hubble Space Telescope.

AskERIC Lesson Plans

http://ericir.syr.edu/Virtual/Lessons/Science/

AskERIC Lesson Plans provides a collection of science lesson plans contributed by teachers for Grades K-12. Topics include agriculture, biological and life sciences, earth science, physical sciences, space sciences, and technology. Each lesson plan features an overview, purpose, objectives, activities, and resource materials.

Athena

http://athena.wednet.edu/

Athena is a joint project of NASA and SAIC for Grades K-12. The site features a collection of online science lessons and activities. Topics include oceans, earth, weather, atmosphere, space, and astronomy. For a list of classroom activities, click What's New?

The Awesome Library: Science Lesson Plans

www.neat-schoolhouse.org/Library/
Materials_Search/Lesson_Plans/Science.html

The Awesome Library: Science Lesson Plans contains a collection of hundreds of science lesson plans for Grades K-12.

Big Sky Science Gopher Menu

gopher://bvsd.k12.co.us:70/11/
Educational_Resources/Lesson_Plans/
Big%20Sky/science/

Big Sky Science Gopher Menu provides more than 200 science lesson plans for Grades K-12. Among its topics are color mixing, orbital paths, soil erosion, blood circulation, bird study, and crystals.

Biology Lessons for Teachers

http://public.sdsu.edu/NaturalSciences/

Biology Lessons for Teachers, contributed by students at San Diego State University, features a collection of biology lesson plans for use in elementary school classrooms. Lessons part 1 covers molecules and cells, and lessons part 2 population biology.

Birds: Our Environmental Indicators

http://nceet.snre.umich.edu/Curriculum/
toc.html

Birds: Our Environmental Indicators, from Earth Generation's New York Educator's Guide, provides 10 complete curriculum plans for junior high students investigating environmental issues relevant to the Great Lakes region.

CEC Lesson Plans

www.col-ed.org/cur/

CEC Lesson Plans, sponsored by the Columbia Education Center in Portland, Oregon, features a wide variety of lesson plans created by teachers for use in their own classrooms. To find science plans, scroll to Science and click Elementary (K-5), Intermediate (6-8), or High School (9-12).

Center for Science Education

http://cse.ssl.berkeley.edu/

The **Center for Science Education** at the U.C. Berkeley Space Science Laboratory provides a collection of SEGway lesson plans for the study of space science, sun and earth, and the solar system in Grades 4-12. To find these plans, click Science Education Gateway. The site also includes online interactive lessons on comets, light, and spectra.

Cody's Science Education Zone

http://ousdmail.ousd.k12.ca.us/~codypren/
CSEZ_Home.htm

Cody's Science Education Zone provides a variety of lesson plans prepared by Anthony Cody, a middle school science teacher in Oakland, California.

Connections+

www.mcrel.org/resources/plus/

Connections+ consists of Internet resources for lesson plans, activities, and curriculum resources. The site is provided by Mid-Continent Regional Educational Laboratory (McREL). K-12 science teachers can select from among these topics: Space and Astronomy, Primates, Chemistry, No Life on Mars?, All About Insects, The Third Domain, Genetics and Disease, Solar Energy, and Craters: How They Form.

CNF Beetle Survey

www.schoolnet.ca/vp-pv/ladybug/e/ladybuge/

Canadian Nature Federation (CNF) Lady Beetle Survey provides lesson plans, printable student activity sheets, background information, and pictures of different lady beetles. The material is appropriate for students in Grades 4-8. To find these resources, click Teacher's Kit.

Dow/NSTA Summer Workshop

http://thechalkboard.com/NSTA.html

Dow/NSTA Summer Workshop provides a collection of chemistry lessons and activities for Grades 9-12 developed by teachers participating in workshops from 1995 through 1997.

Earth Science Lesson Plans and Activities

http://nesen.unl.edu/activities/lesacttoc.html

The Nebraska Earth Science Education Network at the University of Nebraska (Lincoln) provides a collection of lesson plans and activities developed by teachers for K-12 classrooms. Topics range from geology to water to soils to weather. Activities are categorized by grade level and topic.

Educate the Children: Lesson Plans

www.educate.org.uk/lessons.htm

Educate the Children provides a collection of hundreds of lesson plans and worksheets contributed by teachers for Grades K-12. Click Science to find more than 65 lesson plans.

Education World: Science Lesson Plans

http://db.education-world.com/perl/browse?cat_id=1878

Education World, sponsored by American Fidelity Services, provides nearly 225 science lesson plans for Grades K-12. Links include Agriculture, Life Science, Natural History, Physical Science, Space, and Technology.

EE Link: Classroom Resources-Directories

http://eelink.net/classroomresources-directories.html

EE Link provides a searchable collection of environmental education sites organized by topic. Many sites offer lesson plans and activities for K-12. Topics (see the left panel) include fresh water, oceans and coasts, air and climate, endangered species, toxics and waste management, wildlife and biodiversity, and endangered species.

ENC: Lessons and Activities—Science

www.enc.org/classroom/lessons/nf_lessci.htm

The Eisenhower Clearinghouse for Mathematics and Science Education (ENC) provides a collection of sites with science lesson plans and activities for Grades K-12.

Encarta Lesson Collection

www.encarta.msn.com/schoolhouse/lessons/

Encarta Lesson Collection offers a collection of lesson plans contributed by K-12 teachers in various subject areas. To find science plans, click Science.

Endangered Species in Endangered Spaces

http://rbcm1.rbcm.gov.bc.ca/end_species/es_plans/es_plans.html

Endangered Species in Endangered Spaces contains a collection of more than 25 lesson plans, prepared by Carol Thomson of Okanagan College, about endangered animals in British Columbia. Although these lessons were designed for Canadian students, they will fit into any environmental education curriculum for Grades 2-7.

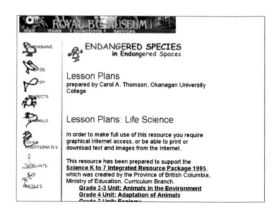

Educational Resources in Science

www.cln.org/subjects/science.html

British Columbia's Community Learning Network provides lesson plans and teaching tips for a variety of subject areas in science. To find this collection of resources suitable for Grades K-12, scroll to Instructional Materials.

The EnviroLink Library

www.envirolink.org/library/

The EnviroLink Library provides a searchable collection of environmental educational resources for Grades K-12. The link features an alphabetical list of lesson plans, activities, and other resources.

Explore Our Resources

www.sln.org/resources/

Explore Our Resources, for Grades K-6, contains a collection of online science lessons and activities contributed by 12 international museums in the Science Learning Network (SLN). Among the topics are acids and bases, El Niño, science of balloons, physics of water fountains, hurricanes, wind, volcanoes, cow's eye dissection, and light, shadow, and images.

Explorer

http://explorer.scrtec.org/explorer/

Explorer offers a large collection of science lesson plans and activities for Grades K-12. Click Natural Sciences Curriculum to find plans for general science, life science, physical science, earth science, and common themes. You can also search for specific science lesson plans in the Explorer database.

Florida Aquarium: Hands On

www2.sptimes.com/aquarium/FA.4.html

The Florida Aquarium provides hands-on lessons and other resources for wannabe marine biologists of all ages. The site also features background information for teachers.

Florida Center for Instructional Technology

http://fcit.coedu.usf.edu/

Florida Center for Instructional Technology (FCIT), located at the University of South Florida, provides lesson plans and instructional materials for Grades K-12. Select Lesson Plans for Technology, click Search for Lessons, and then click by subject to find science plans.

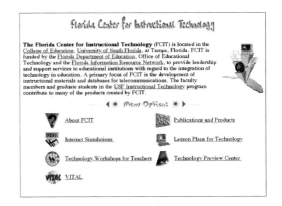

Frank Potter's Science Gems

www-sci.lib.uci.edu/SEP/CTS/

Frank Potter's Science Gems contains hundreds of science resources sorted by category, topic, and grade level useful for teachers and students in Grades K-12. To find Internet-based lesson plans contributed by teachers, scroll to Special Resource Links and click K-12 Science Lesson Plans - '98 or K-12 Science Lesson Plans - '97.

From A Distance

wwwedu.ssc.nasa.gov/ltp/LessonPlans/
about_the_lesson_plans.htm

John C. Stennis Space Center's **From A Distance**,
part of the NASA Learning Technologies Project,
contains a collection of Internet-based lesson
plans on remote sensing developed by teachers for
K-12.

Gateway to Educational Materials (GEM)

www.thegateway.org/

GEM, sponsored by the U.S. Department of
Education, provides access to hundreds of lesson
plans on the Internet, curriculum units, and other
education resources for Grades K-12. To find a list
of science plans, select Browse Subject Lists and
click Science.

GCRIO: It's Elementary

www.gcrio.org/edu/elementary/itselem.html

The **U.S. Global Change Research Information
Office (GCRIO)** provides a variety of
environmental lesson plans for Grades K-8.

The Hitchhikers Guide to Model Rocketry

http://library.advanced.org/10568/

The Hitchhikers Guide to Model Rocketry
provides an online, step-by-step tutorial that
middle school students can use to build and
design their first rockets. The site includes
information on the principles of scientific rocketry
in the Aerodynamics section, as well as other
related links.

Imagine the Universe!

http://imagine.gsfc.nasa.gov/

Imagine the Universe!, created by the High-Energy
Astrophysics Science Archive Research Center
(HEASARC), provides math and science lesson
plans and other resources about astronomy and
space exploration for high school students. To
find the plans contributed by teachers, click
Teachers Corner. The site also includes Ask a
NASA Scientist service, an online dictionary of
astrophysics terms, and related links.

Impact of Shoemaker-Levy 9 Lesson Plan

www.smplanet.com/science/science.html

Impact of Shoemaker-Levy 9 Lesson Plan
contains an online unit of space and astronomy
lessons for middle school students.

Insects!

www.minnetonka.k12.mn.us/SCHOOLS/
groveland/insect.proj/insects.html

Insects!, an Internet-based project, provides a
detailed lesson plan and student worksheets for
studying insects in Grades K-5.

Insects in the Classroom: Bugs as Teaching Tools for All Ages

http://entowww.tamu.edu/academic/ucourses/ento489/insects.html

Texas A&M University's **Insects in the Classroom** contains course activities, a section that includes a collection of K-12 lesson plans organized by age, grade level, and topic for Grades K-12. Included are activity card ideas providing short, hands-on projects involving entomology.

Jet Propulsion Laboratory

www.jpl.nasa.gov/

Jet Propulsion Laboratory (JPL) offers a wealth of earth and space science curriculum resources for students and teachers in Grades K-12. To find lesson plans and other materials, click Education.

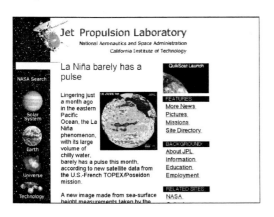

John Glenn, American Hero

www.pbs.org/kcet/johnglenn/

John Glenn, American Hero, a companion site to the PBS program, provides a detailed look at STS-95, a collection of cross-curricular lesson plans and interactive space games, and considers the future of space flight in the 21st century, including the International Space Station. The site is suitable for Grades 5-12.

The K-8 Aeronautics Internet Textbook

http://wings.ucdavis.edu/

The **K-8 Aeronautics Internet Textbook**, developed by Cislunar Aerospace, provides a comprehensive study of the science of aeronautics for elementary and middle school students over the Internet. The text has various reading levels and a Spanish version. The site includes lesson plans with fun experiments and exercises to help students understand the contents of the textbook and also a variety of cross-curriculum activities. The Scientists and Engineers' Guide features a list of more than 36 experiments that can be used in any K-8 science curriculum.

K-12 Weather Curriculum

http://groundhog.sprl.umich.edu/curriculum/

K-12 Weather Curriculum, from the University of Michigan's Weather Underground, contains online lessons and activities for weather, hurricanes, and smog.

Langley Distributed Active Archive Center

http://eosweb.larc.nasa.gov/education/Erb_Intro.html

The NASA **Langley Distributed Active Archive Center** provides a collection of cross-curricular earth science lesson plans, experiments, and follow-up activities to help middle school students learn about the warming up and the cooling down atmospheric conditions. The site includes a glossary and other resources.

Lesson Index

www.crpc.rice.edu/CRPC/GT/dawsonm/lesindex.htm

Marcella Dawson provides a collection of earth, life science, physics lessons, and Web activities she authored for students in Grades 6-12.

The Lesson Plans Page

www.lessonplanspage.com/

The Lesson Plans Page, by Kyle Yamnitz, contains hundreds of lesson plans, including science for Grades K-6.

The Library in the Sky

www.nwrel.org/sky/

The Library in the Sky, provided by Northwest Regional Educational Laboratory (NWREL), contains hundreds of K-12 lesson plans for a variety of subject areas. To find science plans, choose Teacher Resources, select Lesson Plans, and click Science.

McREL: Lesson Plans and Activities

www.mcrel.org/resources/links/lesson.asp

McREL: Lesson Plans and Activities, gathered by Mid-Continent Regional Educational Laboratory (McREL), contains a collection of science lesson plan sites for Grades K-12.

Miami Museum of Science: Online Resources

www.miamisci.org/www/sln.html

Miami Museum of Science provides a variety of online resources and activities for students in Grades 3-8. The pH Factor introduces acids and bases; the Atoms Family contains activities about energy concepts; Hurricane: Storm Science teaches about hurricanes from the inside out; and Ecolinks features environmental information, ideas, and research online.

Minnetonka Elementary Science Center

www.minnetonka.k12.mn.us/support/science/index.shtml

The **Minnetonka Elementary Science Center** provides a collection of lesson plans for Grades K-5. To find them, scroll and click Minnetonka Teacher Information. Now scroll to Science Enrichment/Lesson Plans and choose the grade level you want. You'll also find more classroom activities for science in Teacher Tools.

NASA Glenn Learning Technologies Project

www.grc.nasa.gov/WWW/K-12/

NASA Glenn Learning Technologies Project provides a wide variety of aeronautic resources and lesson plans for students in Grades 7-12.

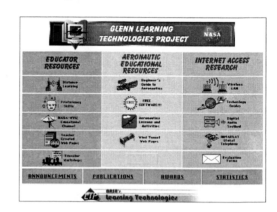

NESEN Lesson Plans & Activities

http://nesen.unl.edu/activities/active1.html

NESEN Lesson Plans & Activities provides a collection of lesson plans and activities for Grades 5-12 developed by teachers participating in Nebraska Earth Science Education Network Summer Workshops. Topics include astronomy, geology, soils, water, and weather.

Newton's Apple

http://ericir.syr.edu/Projects/Newton/

Newton's Apple, for Grades 4-8, features a collection of more than 120 science lessons from seasons 9 through 15 of the award-winning PBS television series. The lessons cover a wide variety of science topics and can be used independently of the TV program. The site also includes an alphabetical list of all of the lessons.

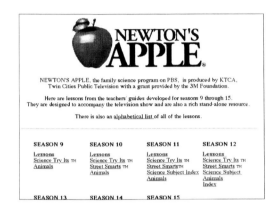

NSTA's Scope, Sequence & Coordination Project

www.gsh.org/nsta/

NSTA's Scope, Sequence & Coordination Project contains more than 100 science micro-units for biology, chemistry, earth/space, and physics for students in Grades 9-12. To find the micro-units organized by topics, click Explore. To find a list of individual micro-units, click Browse. You can also search for specific micro-units.

Ocean Planet

http://seawifs.gsfc.nasa.gov/ocean_planet.html

Ocean Planet, for Grades K-12, is a Smithsonian Institution exhibit containing a collection of lesson plans and other online resources for teaching about marine life. To find the plans, click Enter the Exhibition Here, scroll and then click Educational Materials.

Physical Science Activity Manual

http://cesme.utm.edu/resources/science/PSAM.html

The **Physical Science Activity Manual**, provided by the Center for Excellence in Science and Mathematics Education (CESME) at UTM, features 34 hands-on science lesson activities for Grades 8-10. Topics include the learning cycle, density, physical and chemical properties, mixtures, Newton's three Laws, and air pressure.

Physics 98 Institute Lesson Plans

www.owu.edu/%7emggrote/phys98/lessons.html

Physics 98 contains 20 high school physics lesson plans developed by Ohio teachers attending a summer institute held at Ohio Wesleyan University.

Project Galileo: Bringing Jupiter to Earth

www.jpl.nasa.gov/galileo/

Project Galileo: Bringing Jupiter to Earth provides an assortment of lessons and activities on the spacecraft probe for Grades 5-12. To find these resources, scroll and select Online From Jupiter.

Project Primary

www.owu.edu/~mggrote/pp/

Project Primary provides a collection of hands-on science investigations developed by Ohio Wesleyan University science professors for teachers in Grades K-3. Included are activities for botany, chemistry, geology, physics, and zoology.

The Rainforest Workshop

http://kids.osd.wednet.edu/Marshall/
rainforest_home_page.html

The Rainforest Workshop, for middle school students, provides a variety of lesson plans and activities about temperate and tropical rain forests. To find these plans, click Educational Resources and scroll to Lesson Plans and Activities.

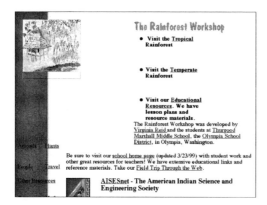

SciCentral: Lesson Plans

www.scicentral.com/K-12/K-lesson.html

SciCentral provides a collection of science sites with hundreds of lesson plans for Grades K-12.

Science Lessons by Subject

www.eecs.umich.edu/~coalitn/sciedoutreach/
funexperiments/agesubject/subject.html

The Southeastern Michigan Math-Science Learning Coalition provides a collection of lessons and experiments for astronomy, biology, chemistry, earth science, and physical science. Lessons are also sorted by age group from early elementary to high school.

SCORE Science: Lessons and Activities

http://scorescience.humboldt.k12.ca.us/fast/
teachers/lessons.htm

SCORE Science, part of the Schools of California Online Resource for Educators, provides a searchable database of lesson plans and activities linked to the California content science standards for Grades K-12. To find the complete list of the plans, select All Grades and All Subjects and click Show Lessons.

SeaWorld/Busch Gardens Educational Resources

www.seaworld.org/teacherguides/
teacherguides.html

SeaWorld/Busch Gardens provides a collection of K-12 teacher's guides with lessons and hands-on activities for teaching about animals and the environment. To find more classroom activities, scroll to the bottom of the page.

SETI Institute Sample Lessons

www.seti-inst.edu/litu-sample-top.html

Search for Extraterrestrial Intelligence (SETI) Institute offers sample lessons from its Life in the Universe Curriculum Project for elementary and middle school students.

SMILE Program Biology Index

www.iit.edu/~smile/biolinde.html

The **Science and Mathematics Initiative for Learning Enhancement (SMILE)** program, maintained by the Illinois Institute of Technology, features more than 200 biology lesson plans developed by teachers for Grades K-12. Topics include anatomy and physiology, zoology, botany, microbiology, environmental studies and ecology, biochemistry, and general biology. Each plan includes objectives, the materials needed, suggested strategy, and expected outcomes.

SMILE Program Chemistry Index

www.iit.edu/~smile/cheminde.html

The **Science and Mathematics Initiative for Learning Enhancement (SMILE)** program, maintained by the Illinois Institute of Technology, features more than 200 chemistry lesson plans developed by teachers for Grades K-12. Topics include basic tools and principles, atomic and molecular structure, states of matter, chemical reactions, chemistry of elements, compounds, and materials. Each plan includes objectives, the materials needed, suggested strategy, and expected outcomes.

SMILE Program Physics Index

www.iit.edu/~smile/physinde.html

The **Science and Mathematics Initiative for Learning Enhancement (SMILE)** program, maintained by the Illinois Institute of Technology, features more 200 physics lesson plans developed by teachers for Grades K-12. Topics include matter, mechanics, fluids, electricity and magnetism, waves, sound and optics, and miscellaneous. Each plan includes objectives, the materials needed, suggested strategy, and expected outcomes.

Smithsonian Education: Lesson Plans

http://educate.si.edu/resources/lessons/lessons.html

The Smithsonian Office of Elementary and Secondary Education provides a collection of classroom-ready lesson plans and activities integrating science with other curriculum areas in Grades K-6.

Spaceborne Imaging Radar-C Education

http://ericir.syr.edu/Projects/NASA/nasa.html

Spaceborne Imaging Radar-C Education (SIR-CED) is the latest generation of imaging radars produced by JPL for NASA. This site offers a Teacher's Resource Guide and a Lesson Guide for middle school and high school students and teachers.

STELLAR

http://stellar.arc.nasa.gov/stellar/

The **Science Training for Enhancing Leadership and Learning Through Accomplishments in Research (STELLAR)**, sponsored by the NASA Ames Research Center, provides lesson plans and hands-on activities developed by teachers for the study of space life sciences in Grades K-12.

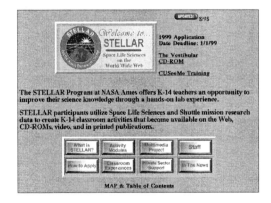

Summer Research Program for NYC Science Teachers

http://cait.cpmc.columbia.edu/dept/physio/

Columbia University's **Summer Research Program for NYC Science Teachers** contains a collection of laboratory lesson plans from 1995-98 for Grades 9-12. These plans were developed by the participating teachers.

Teacher-Developed Earth and Space Science Lessons and Classroom Activities

http://w3.cea.berkeley.edu/Education/lessons/
lessons_teacherdeveloped.html

Teacher-Developed Earth and Space Science Lessons and Classroom Activities, from the University of California, Berkeley, is a collection of science lesson plans for a variety of topics, including weather, satellites, auroras, and earthquakes. The plans are appropriate for students in Grades 4-12.

Teachnet.Com

www.teachnet.com/

Teachnet.Com designed by teachers for K-12 teachers, offers science lesson ideas for biology, earth, physics, scientific method, space and time, weather, and general areas.

TeachersFirst Web Content Matrix

www.teachersfirst.com/matrix-f.htm

TeachersFirst Web Content Matrix, provided by the Network for Instructional Television (NITV), offers a collection of lesson plans at the elementary, middle, and high school levels. To find science plans, scroll to a science subject in the table, and click on lesson plans.

TEAMS Distance Learning: K-12 Lesson Plans

http://teams.lacoe.edu/documentation/places/
lessons.html

TEAMS Distance Learning, maintained by the Los Angeles County Office of Education, provides a collection of lessons plan sites for Grades K-12 organized by subject. To find science lesson plans, click Science.

Using Live Insects in Elementary Classrooms for Early Lessons in Life

http://insected.arizona.edu/uli.htm

The Center for Insect Science Education at the University of Arizona provides a collection of 20 printable integrated lesson plans with science and math activities that use live insects for primary grade children. These lessons introduce health topics to children and are aligned with National Science Education Standards (NSES).

Volcano Lesson Plans

http://volcano.und.nodak.edu/vwdocs/
vwlessons/lesson.html

Volcano World offers volcano-related lessons and classroom activities for Grades 4-12.

Weather Here and There

www.ncsa.uiuc.edu/edu/RSE/RSEred/
WeatherHome.html

Weather Here and There is an interactive weather unit incorporating hands-on, collaborative problem-solving activities for students in Grades 4-6.

BASIC OVERVIEW OF UNIT

WEATHER HERE AND THERE is an integrated weather unit which incorporates interaction with the Internet and hands-on collaborative, problem solving activites for students in grades four through six. This unit is divided into six lessons. The lessons integrate math, science, geography, and language arts in the process of teaching and learning about weather phenomena. Students will become involved in collaborative problem solving using e-mail as well as through joining projects offered via the Internet. *The Global Education Project* will help students see the relevance of science by interacting with scientists and other students across the world, as they collaborate in the study of weather in their environment.

The first three lessons focus on learning basic meteorological concepts about weather elements, how to take measurements using appropriate weather instruments, and recognizing basic weather trends and patterns.

The Weather Unit

http://faldo.atmos.uiuc.edu/WEATHER/
weather.html

The Weather Unit is a collection of thematic lesson plans for Grades 2-4. It integrates the study of weather into all curricular areas. Click Science to find 14 science lessons, including Water Cycle, Rain Game, and Light and Heat.

WeatherEye

http://weathereye.kgan.com/

WeatherEye, created and maintained by Scott Hall and Roger Evans of KGAN Newschannel 2 in Cedar Rapids, Iowa, features lesson plans, experiments, and other online resources for the study of weather in Grades K-12.

Whales: A Thematic Web Unit

http://curry.edschool.Virginia.EDU/go/Whales/

Whales: A Thematic Web Unit is an integrated curriculum unit for use in Grades 4-8. It provides cooperative lesson plans, teacher resources, and interactive student activities and projects. Links to related sites are also included.

Wind: Our Fierce Friend

http://sln.fi.edu/tfi/units/energy/wind.html

Wind: Our Fierce Friend, developed at the Franklin Institute Science Museum, is an interactive collaborative unit that investigates the science of wind energy. It contains lessons and activities for Grades 4-6 and includes student contributions from online schools.

Year Long Project

www.ed.uiuc.edu/ylp/units.html

The College of Education's **Year Long Project** contains a collection of exemplary science units prepared by the preservice teachers from 1994 to 1998 at the University of Illinois, Urbana-Champaign. Science topics include the five senses, bats, electricity, insects, dinosaurs, rocks, vertebrates, simple machines, and weather,

Amateur Science

www.eskimo.com/~billb/amasci.html

Amateur Science contains hundreds of science activities, experiments, and projects for students and teachers in Grades 4-12.

The Annenberg/CPB Project Exhibits Collection

www.learner.org/exhibits/

The **Annenberg/CPB Project Exhibits Collection** covers a list of multimedia, online, interactive projects to enrich the K-12 curriculum. Science projects include Weather, Amusement Park Physics, Garbage, and Volcanoes.

Astronomy Picture of the Day

http://antwrp.gsfc.nasa.gov/apod/astropix.html

Astronomy Picture of the Day, for Grades K-12, features a new picture of the universe each day with an informative explanation. The site also includes an archive of previous pictures dating back to 1995, a topical picture index, and related educational links.

Bad Science

www.ems.psu.edu/~fraser/BadScience.html

Bad Science, maintained by Alistair B. Fraser, dispels many popular misconceptions about science. The site, suitable for Grades K-12, provides links to astronomy, chemistry, meteorology, and physics sites that attempt to sensitize teachers and students to examples of the "bad science" often taught in schools and universities and offered in popular articles and some textbooks.

Beakman's Electric Motor

http://fly.hiwaay.net/~palmer/motor.html

Chris Palmer's **Beakman's Electric Motor** provides simple illustrated directions that show kids in Grades 4-9 how to make an electric motor from ordinary household items. Scroll to Other Links to find a good Spanish translation of this site.

Biology Project

www.biology.arizona.edu/

The **Biology Project**, developed at the University of Arizona, is an interactive online resource for learning biology suitable for AP biology high school students. Topics consist of biochemistry, cell biology, chemicals and human health, immunology, Mendelian genetics as well as cell, human, and molecular biology. Several of the topics include Spanish versions.

Bizarre Stuff You Can Make in Your Kitchen

http://freeweb.pdq.net/headstrong/

Bizarre Stuff You Can Make in Your Kitchen, created by Brian Carusella for Grades 3-9, provides a growing warehouse of science projects and experiments from clouds in a bottle to making an electric motor. You can view all the projects by category or in an alphabetical index.

CBC 4 Kids` Laboratory

www.cbc4kids.ca/regular/the-lab/

Canadian Broadcasting Corporation provides a wide variety of engaging science activities for Grades 2-6. Kids can take a virtual trip into space exploring the planets, play space games, or find answers to puzzling questions in the universe. They can also take fun science quizzes discovering weird news from the world of science, do their own science experiments, make a paper airplane, or investigate the Big Bang.

CELLS Alive!

www.cellsalive.com/

CELLS Alive! provides information on viruses, bacteria, human cells, and parasites for Grades 7-12. The site includes images and videos of micro-organisms that make you sick, and the blood cells that do battle to keep you well, such as white blood cells attacking an invader. You'll find biocams for viewing biological activity in real time and links to sites offering further information on microbiology, infectious diseases, and cell biology.

Chemistry Teacher Support

www.lynx-ltd.org/chemistry/index.html

Chemistry Teacher Support, created by James Aldridge, contains useful links for high school teachers to such topics as Chemistry I, AP Chemistry, Internet Chemistry Resources, Things We're Looking For, and ChemNotes.

Comets and Meteor Showers

http://comets.amsmeteors.org/

Gary Kronk's **Comets and Meteor Showers**, contains information and pictures of comets and meteors for Grades 5-12.

CoVis Geosciences

www.covis.nwu.edu/Geosciences/

CoVis Geosciences is an Internet project that involves thousands of students, more than a hundred teachers, and dozens of researchers and scientists working to improve science education in middle and high schools. The site includes interactive classroom projects for water quality, land use, weather, global warming, and soil science.

Discover Magazine

www.discover.com/

Discover Magazine provides online, in a readable style for high school students and teachers, current and past issues, a picture gallery, Web picks and related sites, and the latest science news. The site also includes the Ask Discover feature where you can get answers to your science questions from expert scientists.

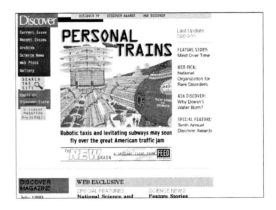

Discovery Channel Online

www.discovery.com/

Discovery Channel Online provides a treasure trove of science curriculum activities for Grades 4-12. You can listen to online or read many interesting stories, take part in daring expeditions, view live cams, or use the guides to find information about animals, extreme weather, space, and other science topics.

Earth & Sky Radio Series

www.earthsky.com/

Earth & Sky Radio Series is a daily, two-minute radio science program for students in Grades 6-12. It can be heard through RealAudio and features popular science topics, including climate and earthquakes. The site also includes a Teacher's Lounge with tips for using Earth & Sky in your classroom and a list of Web resources, such as Ask the Experts page. In addition, kids will find fun science activities.

Earthquake Information from the USGS

http://quake.wr.usgs.gov/

The United States Geological Survey (USGS) provides daily and weekly quake reports, geophysical information on earthquakes, and other background information.

The Electric Club

www.schoolnet.ca/general/electric-club/e/

The Electric Club presents an activities handbook of 37 experiments and projects in electricity and electronics for Grades 5-12. Each of the activities includes a link to Connections, Challenge, Flash Fact, and Teacher's Notes.

The Electronic Zoo

http://netvet.wustl.edu/e-zoo.htm

Ken Boschert's **Electronic Zoo** features a comprehensive catalog of pictures and information about animals for Grades K-12. Scroll and click Animals to find hundreds of animal resources with 22 classifications, from amphibians to zoo animals.

ENC Online

www.enc.org/fr_index.htm

The **Eisenhower National Clearinghouse (ENC)** provides K-12 teachers with a central source of information on mathematics and science curriculum materials. The site offers online publications; recommended mathematics and science lessons, activities, and Internet sites; ideas for educational reform concerning equity; and standards and frameworks.

Energy Quest

www.energy.ca.gov/education/index.html

Energy Quest, from the California Energy Commission, provides a vast collection of activities, organized by difficulty levels, for teaching about energy in Grades K-12. Scroll and click Science Projects, Percy's Puzzles, or Poor Richard's Energy Almanac to find some of these classroom activities.

The Exploratorium Science Snacks

www.exploratorium.edu/snacks/snackintro.html

The Exploratorium Science Snacks provides an online collection of hundreds of experiments designed by science teachers for Grades 4-12. The experiments, adapted from the *Hands-On Sciences* books published by the Exploratorium Museum in San Francisco, include such topics as blue sky, charge and carry, Doppler effect, electroscope, and vector toys. All the snacks can be viewed in an alphabetical list or by subject area.

Explore Science

www.explorescience.com/

Raman Pfaff's **Explore Science** is a multimedia extravaganza illustrating the laws of physics for students in Grades 7-12. It is a shockwave-laden experience of sights, sounds, and interaction with scientific theory. The site provides a collection of interactive explorations for astronomy, mechanics, electricity and magnetism, life science, waves, optics, and other science topics.

Explore the GLOBE Program

www.globe.gov/fsl/welcome.html

Global Learning and Observations to Benefit the Environment (GLOBE) is a worldwide network of students, teachers, and scientists working together to study and understand the global environment. Students and teachers from more than 7,000 schools in more than 80 countries are working with research scientists to learn more about our planet. Research topics include atmosphere, biology, global positioning, hydrology, and soil investigations.

Exploring Planets in the Classroom

www.soest.hawaii.edu/SPACEGRANT/class_acts/

Exploring Planets in the Classroom, for Grades 5-12, contains more than 25 classroom-ready pages of hands-on activities for geology, earth, and planetary sciences.

More than 25 hands-on science activities are provided in classroom-ready pages for both teachers and students for exploring Earth, the planets, geology, and space sciences.

The Faces of Science: African Americans in the Sciences

www.lib.lsu.edu/lib/chem/display/faces.html

The Faces of Science: African Americans in the Sciences, prepared by Louisiana State University, presents nearly 100 profiles of African Americans who have contributed to the advancement of science and engineering. Profiles are grouped by academic discipline and arranged in an alphabetical list. The site is appropriate for students in Grades 5-12.

Family Explorer

www.webcom.com/safezone/FE/

Family Explorer is a monthly newsletter containing hands-on science and nature activities for students in Grades K-6. To find sample activities from recent and past issues of Family Explorer, click Feature or Activities.

Food Zone

http://kauai.cudenver.edu:3010/

The **Food Zone** is an interactive site designed for the Grades 7-12 science classroom. Topics included are nutrition and an overview of the digestive system, including some in-depth discussion. Also included are intermediate and advanced experiments and quizzes designed to test your knowledge.

The Froggy Page

http://frog.simplenet.com/froggy/

The Froggy Page, for Grades K-12, is a comprehensive collection of resources about frogs. It includes pictures, sounds, tales, and songs. To find two online dissection projects, scroll to the Scientific Amphibian section of the page, locate Anatomy and Dissection, and click Whole Frog Project and Frog Dissection Tutorial.

Fun Science Gallery

www.funsci.com/

The **Fun Science Gallery**, suitable for Grades 7-12, is a collection of scientific instruments and experiments to make at home or at school. Projects include instructions for making telescopes, microscopes, batteries, sidereal indicators, and several other instruments.

The Hands-On Technology Program

www.galaxy.net/~k12/

The **Hands-On Technology Program** provides a collection of more than 38 experiments and science hands-on activities for the physical, life, and earth sciences in Grades K-8. All the experiments are designed to be done with ordinary, inexpensive materials; and each experiment includes photocopyable sheets, teachers' notes, and a list of materials needed.

The Heart Preview Gallery

http://sln2.fi.edu/biosci/preview/
heartpreview.html

The **Heart Preview Gallery**, created by the Franklin Institute Science Museum, presents an online interactive tour showing how the heart works. It is accompanied by activities suitable for Grades 4-8. To find the activities, click Learn and Do in the picture of the heart. To start the online tour, click Begin Your Tour of the Heart.

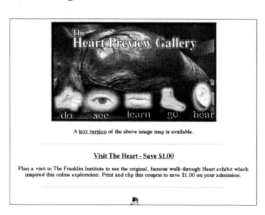

A text version of the above image map is available.

Visit The Heart - Save $1.00

Plan a visit to The Franklin Institute to see the original, famous walk-through Heart exhibit which inspired this online exploration. Print and clip this coupon to save $1.00 on your admission.

Helping Your Child Learn Science

www.ed.gov/pubs/parents/Science/

Helping Your Child Learn Science, prepared by the U.S. Department of Education, provides a collection of hands-on science activities for parents, teachers, and students ages 6-12.

Hewlett Packard Science Experiments

www.discovery-school.org/science.html

Hewlett Packard provides hundreds of activities and experiments for chemistry, motion, light, sound, electricity and magnetism, and other science topics that can be used in any K-8 science curriculum.

How Stuff Works

www.howstuffworks.com/

How Stuff Works, created by Marshall Brain for Grades 4-12, is a series of illustrated articles that explore the workings of devices from cell phones to refrigerators, and explains the principles behind many things from modems to air conditioners. You can ask a question to be answered by the author, read answered questions, or subscribe to a free monthly online newsletter with up-to-date information.

How Things Work

http://howthingswork.virginia.edu/

How Things Work, is based on the book *How Things Work: The Physics of Everyday Life*, by Louis A. Bloomfield, a physics professor at the University of Virginia. He clearly answers What makes an airplane fly?, How do light bulbs work?, Why do microwaves heat things?, and hundreds more science questions. The site, suitable for Grades 7-12, explains physics concepts and laws using everyday life examples from seesaws to copy machines to tape recorders to superconductors to roller coasters. You can submit everyday physics questions and get answers from the author himself.

Hubble Space Telescope Public Pictures

www.stsci.edu/EPA/Pictures.html

Hubble Space Telescope (HST) Public Pictures, for Grades K-12, contains collections of spectacular pictures of celestial objects, each accompanied by brief descriptions. The site includes pictures organized by subject, 1994-1998 releases, HST's Greatest Hits Updated 1990-1998 Picture Gallery, and HST's Greatest Hits 1990-1995 Picture Gallery.

Katerpillars (& Mystery Bugs)

www.uky.edu/Agriculture/Entomology/
ythfacts/entyouth.htm

The University of Kentucky Entomology Department provides a variety of insect projects for elementary school kids. The site also include a teacher/parent category with teaching ideas and materials.

Learning from the Fossil Record

www.ucmp.berkeley.edu/fosrec/fosrec.html

Learning from the Fossil Record provides online resources and a collection of paleontology activities for students and teachers in Grades K-12. Check the standards matrix to find the grade levels identified for each activity.

MAD Scientist Network

www.madsci.org/

The **MAD Scientist Network**, housed at Washington University Medical School in St. Louis, is a collective cranium of scientists from various disciplines providing answers to your questions. From their Ask-A-Scientist archive, you can browse thousands of previously answered questions. In the Mad Labs, you'll find a collection of edible/inedible experiments that require nothing more than rummaging through your kitchen cabinets. The site also provides a comprehensive collection of science sites.

MAST

http://matse1.mse.uiuc.edu/~tw/home.html

Materials Science and Engineering (MAST) project from the University of Illinois, Urbana-Champaign, provides a collection of low-cost laboratory experiments and other resources to teach high school students about the scientific principles of materials. Modules include ceramics, polymers, semiconductors, composites, concrete, metals, and energy. Each module contains lab activities, an equipment list, a glossary, a quiz, and scientific information on the topic.

MathMol K-12 Activity Page

http://cwis.nyu.edu/pages/mathmol/K_12.html

MathMol K-12 Activity Page serves as a starting point for those interested in learning about the field of molecular modeling and its relationship to mathematics.

McREL's Whelmers

www.mcrel.org/whelmers/

McREL's Whelmers are 20 hands-on science activities for Grades K-12 from Steve Jacobs' book *Whelmers*. Included are science activities that will catch the eye and mind of even the most indifferent student. Each experiment has been aligned to the National Science Education Standards.

Microworlds: Exploring the Structure of Materials

www.lbl.gov/MicroWorlds/

Microworlds: Exploring the Structure of Materials is an interactive tour of current research in the materials sciences at Lawrence Berkeley National Laboratory's Advanced Light Source. To start your tour, scroll and click Contents to find online activities appropriate for students at the high school level.

Mr. Biology's High School Bio Website

www.hiline.net/~siremba/

Mr. Biology's Bio High School Bio Website, created by Charles Zaremba, offers online a complete Biology I Curriculum, explanations, worksheets, biological pictures archive, related links, and homework help to high school biology students.

NASA SpaceLink

http://spacelink.nasa.gov/

NASA **SpaceLink**, an aeronautics and space teacher resource since 1988, provides a wealth of online activities for Grades K-12. Click Instructional Materials to find a treasury of classroom resources in the NASA Educational Products and the Curriculum Support links. The site also includes a search engine to help you find educational NASA resources.

NASA's Quest Project: The Internet in the Classroom

http://quest.arc.nasa.gov/

NASA's **Quest Project** provides support and services to K-12 schools, teachers, and students for using the Internet as a basic learning tool. Click Online Interactive Projects to find a list of current and archival collaborative projects.

National Aeronautics and Space Administration

www.nasa.gov/

The **National Aeronautics and Space Administration (NASA)** provides a wealth of science resources for Grades K-12. Among the resources, you'll find featured cool NASA sites. In the panel, you'll also find links to earth and space sites, a collection of NASA sites just for kids, and student and teacher educational resources. To find the site for each of the NASA field centers, click Welcome to NASA Web.

National Science Teachers Association

www.nsta.org/

National Science Teachers Association (NSTA), the leading professional science teaching organization provides innumerable resources for K-12 teachers. The site features information about sponsored publications, programs, and projects and also provides links to other online resources.

NERDS

http://nerds.unl.edu/

Nebraska Educators Really Doing Science (NERDS) houses a library of more than 40 science demos created by teachers for Grades 7-12. To find this collection of experiments for chemistry, physics, and biology, click Teacher Resources. The site also includes an illustrated water rockets unit.

Neuroscience for Kids

http://faculty.washington.edu/chudler/
neurok.html

Neuroscience for Kids, created by Professor Eric H. Chudler of the University of Washington in Seattle for Grades K-7, is designed to help students learn more about the nervous system. Visit the Explore the Nervous System page to get information about the brain, the spinal cord, the neuron, the senses, and other related topics. To help you learn this nervous system information, click Experiments and Activities to find plenty of experiments, a coloring book, activities, and games. Included in this page is a collection of printable brain worksheets and lessons.

New Scientist Planet Science

www.newscientist.com/

New Scientist Planet Science is a companion site for the *New Scientist* magazine. This online magazine contains articles, editorials, letters to the editor, selected science sites (hot spots), bizarre entertaining tales, and other science information on a variety of topics for Grades 9-12. The Last Word, a question-and-answer service, offers a searchable database of more than 600 answered questions on everyday science phenomena. Why is the sky blue? Why does hair turn gray? Do giraffes ever get hit by lightning?

Newton's Apple: Science Try Its

www.pbs.org/ktca/newtons/tryits/

Newton's Apple, the award-winning PBS television series, provides a collection of Science Try Its experiments for Grades 5-8. To find Science Try Its, click SEASON 9, SEASON 10, SEASON 11, SEASON 12, SEASON 13, or SEASON 14.

NEWTON BBS

http://newton.dep.anl.gov/

The Argonne National Laboratory provides an ask-a-scientist service for Grades K-12 with an archive of more than 15,000 previously answered questions from 1991 to the present. The service includes an online form for submitting science questions.

Northeast Fisheries Science Center

www.wh.whoi.edu/noaa.html

Northeast Fisheries Science Center, from Woods Hole Laboratory, provides middle and high school students with resources for learning about our living oceans. Click Fish Facts to find A Bouillabaisse of Fascinating Facts About Fish, including thousands of photos from the late 1800s to the present.

NOVA Online

www.pbs.org/wgbh/nova/

NOVA Online is a valuable resource for science teachers in Grades 6-12. Unlike many Web sites that promote TV shows, this site presents hundreds of well-written articles derived from this venerable public television documentary series, including images and video clips. In addition, teachers will find lots of lesson ideas and online activities that can be used without the video tapes of the shows.

NSSDC Photo Gallery

http://nssdc.gsfc.nasa.gov/photo_gallery/

NSSDC (National Space Science Data Center) Photo Gallery contains hundreds of spectacular and popular photos of planetary, astronomical, and related objects for students in Grades 4-12. The site also includes indexes of images of the solar system, objects taken by the Galileo spacecraft, the Hubble Space Telescope, and the Voyager 1 and 2 spacecrafts.

Nye Labs Online

http://nyelabs.kcts.org/flash_go.html

Nye Labs Online, the Internet home of Bill Nye for Grades 4-8, now requires Macromedia's free Shockwave plug-in to access many of its updated features. Demo of the Day and Home Demos provide a collection of experiments that teachers can print and recopy for their classrooms. Other new features include a Teacher's Lounge with information about the shows; a Goodies section with science videos, sounds, and photos; and an Ask Bill Nye service where your science questions are answered weekly. Don't miss the catchy "Do you know thats." Try this one: "If you shouted on the moon, no one would hear you."

Online Educational Resources

http://quest.arc.nasa.gov/OER/

NASA Online Educational Resources (OER), from the High Performance Computing and Communications (HPCC) Office, features a repository of programs for K-12 students. Among the links included are Spotlighted WWW Sites and NASA Internet Educational Resources.

Optics for Kids

www.opticalres.com/kidoptx.html#StartKidOptxl

Optics for Kids contains activities, experiments, and a selected bibliography for understanding the basics of light and lasers. The materials are appropriate for students in Grades 5-8.

Physics 2000

www.colorado.edu/physics/2000/

Physics 2000, from the University of Colorado at Boulder, provides animated science demonstrations for high school science students and teachers. The site takes you on an interactive journey through modern physics that allows you to learn about Einstein's Legacy on X-rays, microwave ovens, lasers, and many other modern devices. You can also visit an Atomic Lab to see some surprising 20th-century physics experiments.

Questacon: Fun Zone

www.questacon.edu.au/fun_zone.html

Questacon, a children's science and technology museum in Canberra, Australia, provides a Fun Zone for elementary school kids. The site includes a collection of hands-on experiments, online space and dinosaur activities, and incredible illusions.

Quick and Easy Activities

www.eecs.umich.edu/~coalitn/sciedoutreach/
funexperiments/quickndirty/quickneasy.html

The Southeastern Michigan Math-Science Learning Coalition provides a collection of more than 200 hands-on activities and fun experiments for Grades K–12. The activities are categorized by preschool, early elementary, later elementary, middle school, and high school levels.

Rain or Shine: Explorations in Meteorology

www.caps.ou.edu/CAPS/teacher.html

The Center for Analysis and Prediction of Storms (CAPS) at the University of Oklahoma provides a variety hands-on activities accompanied by printable worksheets to help K–12 students learn more about meteorology. The site includes a Teacher's Guide and learning modules ranging from The Sun and Our Weather to Wild Weather.

Rainforest Action Network

www.ran.org/ran/intro.html

Rainforest Action Network (RAN) has been working since 1985 to protect the earth's rain forests and support the rights of its inhabitants. RAN's site provides many online science-education resources. Click Kids' Corner to find classroom activities for use in Grades K–8.

Reeko's Mad Scientist Lab: Experiments for Kids of All Ages

www.flash.net/~spartech/ReekoScience/

Reeko's Mad Scientist Lab features a collection of science experiments delivered in an irreverent style for Grades 4–12. Click EXPERIMENTS in the panel on the left side of the screen to find these fun activities sorted by categories from chemistry to sound. The experiments are also organized by skill levels of easy, medium, and hard. For more activities, click More Experiments.

Safari Touch Tank

http://oberon.educ.sfu.ca/projects/safari/
3DTouchTank/3dlib/tank.html

Safari Touch Tank, created at Simon Fraser University for Grades 4–8, is a clickable undersea on-screen aquarium at which kids can click an item to find a description about it, use an online dictionary to learn its definition and pronunciation, see it enlarged, or view a short animation about it. The site includes a gallery of all the images used in the aquarium.

SandlotScience.com

www.SandlotScience.com/

SandlotScience.com is an online collection of colorful optical illusions for Grades 4–12 without a lot of "deep" science. The site includes many interactive demonstrations, science projects, puzzles, and related links.

Science Activities Index

http://sln.fi.edu/tfi/activity/act-summ.html

Science Activities Index, from the Franklin Institute, is a collection of more than 40 K–8 science activities arranged by subject and grade level. Activity topics include heartbeat, the earth bowl, ocean in a bottle, clear as crystal, and spinning satellites.

Science Explorer

www.exploratorium.edu/science_explorer/

Science Explorer from the Exploratorium contains a variety of hands-on activities, with step-by-step instructions, that elementary kids can do at home. At the bottom of the each experiment's page, click on Ken Finn if you want to send him a message about your results and discoveries.

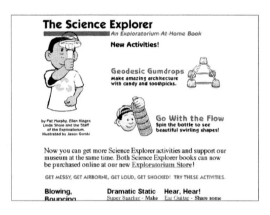

Science Friday Kids Connection

www.npr.org/programs/sfkids/

Science Friday Kids Connection, sponsored by National Public Radio (NPR) and Kidsnet, provides a variety of science-related topics for Grades 6-12. The show archives offers an online library of previous broadcasts that you can listen to through RealAudio. Each episode is accompanied by classroom materials that include a synopsis, selected references, student questions, a class project, experiments, and links to related sites.

Science is Fun

http://scifun.chem.wisc.edu/scifun.html

Bassam Z. Shakhashiri, a professor of chemistry at the University of Wisconsin-Madison, shares the fun of science through home science activities, chemical demonstrations, and general chemistry information for Grades 5-12.

Science Playwiths

www.ozemail.com.au/~macinnis/scifun/

Peter Macinnis' **Science Playwiths** provides a wide variety of fun science experiments that can be made with everyday things for Grades K–8. Topics consist of bubbles, earthy things, electricity and magnetism, fluid flow, gases and liquids, making things, mini-experiments, kitchen chemistry, physics for living things, science quickies, open-ended questions, sight and light things, living things, and sound. Each experiment includes a simple explanation that is linked to "This will help you understand."

Science Resource Center

http://chem.lapeer.org/

Science Resource Center, created by Patrick M. Gormley, provides high school science teachers with demonstrations, laboratory investigations, and teaching tips for chemistry, biology, life science, and physics.

Scientific American

www.sciam.com/

Scientific American contains enhanced versions of print articles, explorations of recent developments in the news, interviews, ask the experts, and much more for students and teachers in Grades 9-12.

SeaWiFS Project

http://seawifs.gsfc.nasa.gov/SEAWIFS.html

SeaWiFS Project, provided by NASA's Goddard Space Flight Center, features a high school Teacher's Guide that includes online activities for the study of ocean color from space. Topics include life in the ocean, the ocean isn't just blue, phytoplankton, the earth, and carbon.

SeaWorld/Busch Gardens Animal Resources

www.seaworld.org/infobook.html

SeaWorld/Busch Gardens offers a wealth of information about animal life and our ecosystems for Grades K-8. Animal Bytes helps kids locate quick information about terrestrial or aquatic animals, Aquatic Safari helps kids find facts about this tropical ecosystem, and Ask Shamu provides answers to the most commonly asked questions about animal life. To find other animal information on such topics as killer whales, sharks, tigers, and tropical forests, click an item in the yellow panel.

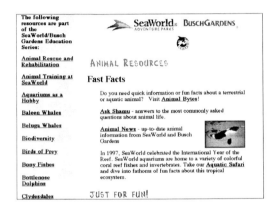

SEDS

www.seds.org/

Students for the Exploration and Development of Space (SEDS), contains a vast array of astronomy and astrophysics resources for Grades 5-12. Included are the multimedia tour of our nine-planet solar system and a galaxy page with more information about the solar system, space sciences, astronauts, and the future.

SERCC Education Center

http://water.dnr.state.sc.us/climate/sercc/education.html

The **Southeast Regional Climate Center (SERCC)** provides a variety of weather resources for Grades 5-9. You'll find weather information by topic; Southern AER, an online quarterly bulletin with interactive student weather activities; a severe weather page, a weather quiz, and links to other weather and environmental sites.

Simple Electric Motor

http://members.tripod.com/simplemotor/

Simple Electric Motor is an award-winning science fair project on the construction of a really neat brushless DC motor for students in Grades 6-12. The site provides complete constructions plans as well as a kit you can buy containing all of the materials necessary to build the motor.

Space Place

http://spaceplace.jpl.nasa.gov/spacepl.htm

The **Space Place** from Jet Propulsion Laboratory (JPL) offers a variety a variety of hands-on earth and space science activities and projects for elementary school kids.

StarChild

http://starchild.gsfc.nasa.gov/

StarChild, created by the NASA Goddard Space Flight Center, is a premiere astronomy resource for teachers and students in Grades K-8. Presented in two levels, it contains pictures and information about our solar system, galaxies, space, the universe, and other astronomy topics.

Thinking Fountain

www.sci.mus.mn.us/sln/

Thinking Fountain, created by the Science Museum of Minnesota, is an interactive mural containing science activities and experiments for students in Grades K-6. Click any item in the mural to explore an activity, or scroll to the bottom of the page and click A to Z for an alphabetical list of all items in the mural.

TRC Activities

www.lerc.nasa.gov/Other_Groups/K-12/TRC/TRCactivities.html

NASA Glenn **Teacher Resource Center (TRC)**, located in Cleveland, Ohio, provides hands-on classroom activities for teaching about aeronautics and rockets in Grades 7-12. TRC also includes an index of space terms.

U.S. Geological Survey's Learning Web

www.usgs.gov/education/

U.S. Geological Survey's Learning Web provides a collection of classroom activities, projects, and earth science resources for Grades K-12.

UT Science Bytes

http://ur.utenn.edu/ut2kids/

UT (University of Tennessee) Science Bytes is a series of online articles about science topics suitable for students in Grades K-12. Among the articles are MarsRocks, Mad About Marmosets, and Rhinos and Tigers and Bears—Oh My!

Vertebrate Animals Hotlist

http://sln.fi.edu/tfi/hotlists/animals.html

Vertebrate Animals Hotlist, prepared by the Franklin Institute, provides students in Grades K-8 with more than 150 links to resources containing information, facts, and pictures about animals.

Views of the Solar System

http://spaceart.com/solar/

Views of the Solar System, created by Calvin J. Hamilton in four languages, is an online guide of the solar system for students in Grades 5-12. The site contains more than 220 Web pages of information and more than 950 pictures and animations of the sun, planets, moons, asteroids, comets, and meteoroids. The Contents link lists all of the site's pages and interactive activities.

Virtual Body

www.medtropolis.com/vbody/

The **Virtual Body** contains a collection of interactive presentations on the functions of the brain, the digestive system, the heart, and the skeleton of the human body for Grades 4-12.

Virtual Frog Dissection Kit

http://george.lbl.gov/vfrog/

Virtual Frog Dissection Kit, designed by the Lawrence Berkeley National Laboratory, provides an interactive dissection of a frog for students in high school biology classes. To learn how to use this kit, scroll and click Tutorial. Students can test their knowledge of frog anatomy by clicking the Virtual Frog Builder Game. The kit is available in a number of languages, including English and Spanish.

Volcano World

http://volcano.und.nodak.edu/

Volcano World is a premiere source of volcano information on the Internet for Grades K-12.

Water Science for Schools

http://ga.water.usgs.gov/edu/

Water Science for Schools, produced by the U.S. Geological Survey, offers information on many aspects of water, along with pictures, data, maps, a glossary, and an interactive center where you can give opinions and test your water knowledge.

WaterWorks

www.omsi.edu/sln/ww/

WaterWorks, from the Oregon Museum of Science and Industry, contains activities for teaching about water pumps, siphons, and the operation of fountains. It also provides information and ideas for building fountains with simple materials.

The Weather Channel

www.weather.com/

The Weather Channel provides forecasts for anywhere in the world. The site also offers weather education resources and classroom activities for Grades 4-12. To view all the site's resources, scroll and click the Site Map.

WebElements

www.webelements.com/

WebElements, created by Mark Winter of the University of Sheffield in England, provides detailed information about every element in the periodic table for students in Grades 7-12.

WhaleNet

http://whale.wheelock.edu

WhaleNet provides a compendium of resources about whales and other marine mammals for students and teachers in Grades K-12.

The Why Files

http://whyfiles.news.wisc.edu/

The Why Files, an online science news journal created by the National Institute for Science Education for Grades 5-12, presents weekly in-depth explorations of the science behind the headlines.

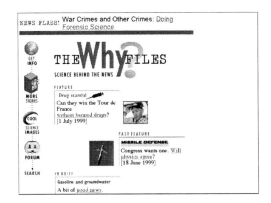

Windows to the Universe

www.windows.umich.edu/

Windows to the Universe provides a rich array of documents, including images, movies, animations, and data sets that explore the earth and space sciences for Grades K-12. The Kids' Space section offers three levels and a variety of interactive activities.

Wonders of Physics

http://sprott.physics.wisc.edu/wop.htm

Physics Professor Clint Sprott provides online a *Physics Demonstrations* sourcebook with dramatic demos for motion, heat, sound, electricity, and other physics topics as well as experiments you can do at home from his popular **Wonders of Physics** program at the University of Wisconsin. To find these materials, scroll to Additional Information. The site is suitable for high school science classes.

WW2010 Online Meteorology Guide

ww2010.atmos.uiuc.edu/(Gh)/guides/

The Weather World 2010, from the University of Illinois at Urbana-Champaign, provides an online meteorology guide featuring a collection of multimedia, Web-based instructional modules for Grades 6-12. Topics include air masses, fronts, clouds, precipitation, El Niño, winds, hurricanes, severe storms, cyclones, and weather forecasting.

WW2010 Projects and Activities

ww2010.atmos.uiuc.edu/(Gh)/guides/

The Weather World 2010, from the University of Illinois at Urbana-Champaign, provides a variety of Collaborative Visualization (CoVis) projects and classroom activities in the atmospheric sciences for Grades 9-12. Topics include pressure, air masses, precipitation, forecasting, and weather symbols. Each student activity is accompanied by a corresponding teacher guide.

You Can

www.youcan.com/

You Can, by Jok R. Church, provides more than 40 science activities in the 50 Terrific ?s section for Grades K-8. Activities in a question-and-answer format include "How does a lever make you stronger?," "Why do I hear weird sounds at night?," "How does yeast make bread rise?," and "What is thunder made out of?" The site also includes exciting interactive demos.

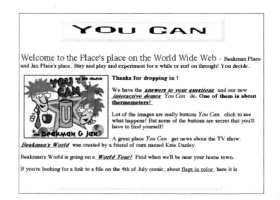

The Yuckiest Site on the Internet

www.nj.com/yucky/

The Yuckiest Site on the Internet, presented by New Jersey Online, features the worlds of worms, cockroaches, and the human body for Grades K-8. The site offers activities, information, and illustrations related to these topics.

Zoom School

www.ZoomSchool.com/

Enchanted Learning Software provides **Zoom School** with comprehensive online books about birds, dinosaurs, whales, sharks, and other science topics. The materials are designed for students of all ages and levels of comprehension. The site includes printable worksheets, interactive quizzes, and dictionaries to accompany the books.

Discovering Dinosaurs

http://dinosaurs.eb.com/dinosaurs/index2.html

Discovering Dinosaurs, from Britannica.com, is an online exhibit about dinosaurs for Grades 5-12. The activity guide introduces you to the dinosaurs as we know them today and shows how theories about them have changed. Click Enter this site to trace the great dinosaur debate through time by traveling down through each theme.

Exploratorium

www.exploratorium.edu/

Exploratorium provides a collection of online interactive exhibits and resources for teachers and students in Grades K-12.

The Franklin Institute Science Museum

http://sln.fi.edu/

The Franklin Institute Science Museum offers a variety of education resources for students and teachers in Grades K-12.

Hands-On Science Centers Worldwide

www.cs.cmu.edu/~mwm/sci.html

Hands-On Science Centers Worldwide is a collection of interactive, public science museums from five continents. The site is appropriate for students in Grades K-12.

John Donohue's National Park Photos

http://anansi.panix.com:80/~wizjd/
cgi-bin/getphoto.cgi

John Donohue's National Park Photos, for Grades K-12, is a collection of photos of America's favorite national parks. Click Slide Show to view 30 of Donohue's favorite photos. To find links to additional resources, scroll to Other Park and Great Outdoors Pages.

National Air and Space Museum

www.nasm.edu/

National Air and Space Museum, for Grades K-12, features a collection of exhibits and online resources about aviation and space science.

Natural History Museum of Los Angeles County

www.nhm.org/

Natural History Museum of Los Angeles County provides an impressive array of online exhibits, kid's stuff, and teacher materials for Grades K-12. Click the site map to find these resources in the Education column.

New Mexico Museum of Natural History and Science

www.nmmnh-abq.mus.nm.us/nmmnh/nmmnh.html

New Mexico Museum of Natural History and Science contains a wide variety of resources for students in Grades K–12. Click Related Web Sites to find links to other online museums. To find classroom materials and activities for dinosaurs and mammals, click Research and Collections.

Science Learning Network

www.sln.org/

Science Learning Network (SLN) is an online collaboration among 12 international science museums providing hands-on activities for K–8 students. Click Explore Our Resources for a collection of interactive exhibits, and click news and links for other science resources from these museums.

Yahoo!: Science Museums and Exhibits

http://dir.yahoo.com/Science/Museums_and_Exhibits/

Yahoo!: Science Museums and Exhibits is a directory of online science museums and exhibits, including aquariums and zoos.

Social Studies

Academy Curricular Exchange: Social Studies, Elementary School (K–5)

http://ofcn.org/cyber.serv/academy/ace/soc/
elem.html

Academy Curricular Exchange: Social Studies, Elementary School (K–5) provides 50 lesson plans for students in the primary grades.

Academy Curricular Exchange: Social Studies, High School (9–12)

http://ofcn.org/cyber.serv/academy/ace/soc/
high.html

Academy Curricular Exchange: Social Studies, High School (9–12) offers 95 lesson plans suitable for the high school level.

Academy Curricular Exchange: Social Studies, Intermediate School (6–8)

http://ofcn.org/cyber.serv/academy/ace/soc/
inter.html

Academy Curricular Exchange: Social Studies, Intermediate School (6–8) features 80 lesson plans appropriate for pupils in middle school.

Anne Frank in the World, 1929–1945: Teacher Workbook

www.uen.org/utahlink/lp_res/AnneFrank.html

Anne Frank in the World, 1929–1945: Teacher Workbook is provided by the Friends of Anne Frank in Utah and the Intermountain West Region. It includes lesson plans and activities for Grades 5-12, readings and overviews, timelines, and a glossary.

AskAsia

www.askasia.org/index.htm

AskAsia, developed by the Asia Society in cooperation with several partners, offers high-quality, carefully selected resources for the classroom. Click For Educators and then Instructional Resources to find lesson plans, readings, and a resource center locator. All lessons, images, and maps have been copyright cleared and can be downloaded to use in the classroom. Lesson plan topics include Global, Asia-General, Asian American, Central Asia, China, India, Indonesia, Japan, Korea, Middle East, Taiwan, and Vietnam.

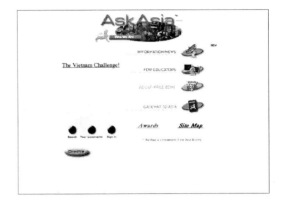

Awesome Library Social Studies Lesson Plans

www.neat-schoolhouse.org/Library/
Materials_Search/Lesson_Plans/
Social_Studies.html

Awesome Library Social Studies Lesson Plans presents a large number of links to a variety of lesson plans representing all areas of the K-12 social studies curriculum.

Beyond the Playing Field: Jackie Robinson, Civil Rights Advocate

www.nara.gov/education/teaching/robinson/
robmain.html

Beyond the Playing Field: Jackie Robinson, Civil Rights Advocate, provided by the National Archives and Records Administration, features nine primary sources (including letters, telegrams, and photos), with accompanying lesson plans related to the documents. The lesson plans include objectives, materials, procedures, and follow up. Also featured are Robinson Quotes.

Big Sky Social Studies Gopher Menu

gopher://bvsd.k12.co.us:70/11/
Educational_Resources/Lesson_Plans/
Big%20Sky/social_studies

Big Sky Social Studies Gopher Menu presents K-12 social studies lesson plans. It includes a large collection for teaching a variety of subjects, including American history, geography, economics, and government.

CEC Lesson Plans

www.col-ed.org/cur/

CEC Lesson Plans, sponsored by the Columbia Education Center based in Portland, Oregon, features a large assortment of lesson plans created by teachers for use in their own classrooms. Click Elementary (K-5), Intermediate (6-8), or High School (9-12) to find lesson plans to fit your needs.

Celebrations: A Social Studies Resource Guide for Elementary Teachers

http://teacherlink.ed.usu.edu/TLresources/
longterm/Byrnes/intro.html

Celebrations: A Social Studies Resource Guide for Elementary Teachers, developed by students at Utah State University, features lesson plans for 50 holidays and celebrations. Included are April Fool's Day, Cambodian New Year, Chinese New Year, Christmas, Cinco de Mayo, Columbus Day, Day of the Dead, Halloween, Hanukkah, Kwanzaa, Martin Luther King Day, Mexican Independence, Ramadan, Rosh Hashanah, and Thanksgiving.

Connections+

www.mcrel.org/resources/plus/

Connections+ consists of K-12 lesson plans, activities, and curriculum resources provided by McREL. Social studies teachers can select from among these topics: Behavioral/Social Studies, Civics, Economics, Geography, History, and Multi-Interdisciplinary for links to lesson plans and activities.

Crossroads: A K-16 American History Curriculum

http://ericir.syr.edu/Virtual/Lessons/
crossroads/

Crossroads: A K-16 American History Curriculum was produced by the Sage Colleges (Troy, New York) and the Niskayuna School District (Niskayuna, New York). The curriculum is composed of 36 units equally distributed among elementary, middle, and high school grade levels. Lesson plans and student worksheets are included.

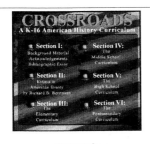

Crossroads
A K-16 American History Curriculum

Background Material I Essays I Elementary Curriculum I
Middle School Curriculum I High School Curriculum I
Postsecondary Curriculum

Curriculum of United States Labor History for Teachers

www.kentlaw.edu/ilhs/curricul.htm

Curriculum of United States Labor History for Teachers, sponsored by the Illinois Labor History Society, features 13 lesson plans that integrate labor history into the U.S. history curriculum from the Colonial period to the present.

EcEdWeb

http://ecedweb.unomaha.edu/teach.htm

EcEdWeb provides lesson plans and curriculum materials from the Economic Education Web site. The site's goal is to provide support for economics education from kindergarten through Grade 12. Teacher's guides, lesson plans, and activities are featured.

Economics and Geography Lessons for 32 Children's Books

www.mcps.k12.md.us/curriculum/socialstd/
Econ_Geog.html

Economics and Geography Lessons for 32 Children's Books was developed by Patricia King Robeson and Barbara Yingling and is sponsored by the Council on Economic Education in Maryland and the Maryland Geographic Alliance. The site provides lesson plans suitable for Grades 1-5. Included are objectives, vocabulary, materials, and teacher background.

Education World Lesson Plans: Social Studies

http://db.education-world.com/perl/
browse?cat_id=1879

Education World Lesson Plans: Social Studies contains more than 150 social studies lesson plans, K-12, selected by Education World.

Florida Geographic Alliance Lesson Plans

http://multimedia2.freac.fsu.edu/fga/
lessonplans.html

Florida Geographic Alliance Lesson Plans, from the Geographic Education and Technology Program of Florida State University, provides lesson plans for studies of various parts of the world (organized by continent).

Golden Legacy: Chinese Historical & Cultural Project Curriculum

www.kqed.org/cell/school/socialstudies/golden/menu.html

Golden Legacy: Chinese Historical & Cultural Project Curriculum provides lesson plans for a variety of topics. These include New Beginnings (Immigration, Chinatowns), Survival (Railroad Building, New Almaden Mine, Agriculture), Daily Life (Clothing, Bound Feet, Queues, Names), Traditions (Celebrations, Symbolism, Lunar Calendar), Education System (Writing System, Abacus, Tangrams, Folktales & Games, Puppetry), and Lasting Legacy (Postage Stamps, Conclusion).

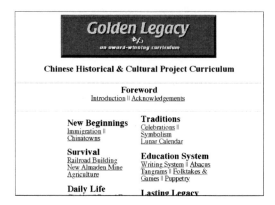

Homework Help

http://talk.startribune.com/cgi-bin/WebX.cgi?homework-14@@.ee6b2b9

Homework Help, sponsored by the Star Tribune Online, is a forum where a secondary student can ask a question about history, geography, government, current events, or other social studies topics. One of the Homework Help teachers who specializes in social studies will post a response.

Internet CNN Newsroom

www.nmis.org/NewsInteractive/CNN/Newsroom/contents.html

Internet CNN Newsroom contains Teacher's Guides for middle and high school teachers to use with CNN's TV Newsroom Program. Teachers can videotape the program while they sleep (1:30 a.m.-2 a.m., Monday-Friday). Each episode usually presents five or six brief news stories with no commercials.

Japan Lessons: Lesson Plans for K-12 Teachers

www.indiana.edu/~japan/japan/mdnjapan/menu.html

Japan Lessons: Lesson Plans for K-12 Teachers contains objectives, materials, suggested classroom time, procedures, extension ideas, teacher background information, and student worksheets. To see all the lesson plans, click the Browse button.

Judges in the Classroom

www.wa.gov/courts/educate/home.htm

Judges in the Classroom was developed under the auspices of the Washington State courts. Although the lesson plans found here were designed to help judges teach in K-12 classrooms, they can be adapted by social studies teachers with an interest in teaching about the law and the Bill of Rights. Click Elementary School Classrooms, Middle School Classrooms, or High School Classrooms to find the appropriate plans.

Lesson Plan Database

www.lennox.k12.ca.us/LPD.html

Lesson Plan Database presents 19 Native American thematic units for elementary pupils. The units were designed by Shayna Gardner of the Lennox (California) School District. Lesson plan topics include Cave Painting, Chumash Village, Sand Painting, Teepee Lesson, Nature Names, and more.

Lesson Plans and Resources for Social Studies Teachers

www.csun.edu/~hcedu013/

Lesson Plans and Resources for Social Studies Teachers includes several hundred social studies lesson plans (K-12), online activities, teaching suggestions for current events lessons, and additional resource materials.

Lesson Plans for Teaching About the Americas

http://ladb.unm.edu/retanet/plans/soc/

Lesson Plans for Teaching About the Americas, provided by RETAnet, presents lesson plans written by secondary teachers. The plans are organized around these topics: Latin America Overview, Mexico, Indigenous Issues, African American and Caribbean Issues, Immigration, Geography, and Miscellaneous Subjects.

Lesson Plans/Classroom Activities for Archaeology Themes

www.ties.k12.mn.us/~mayatch/mq96/lesson/Archaeology/

Lesson Plans/Classroom Activities for Archaeology Themes, from MayaQuest, will help social studies teachers plan fun, hands-on learning activities for Grades 5-8. Featured topics include planting a time capsule or planning an archaeological dig.

Lesson Plans/Classroom Activities for Hieroglyphics Themes

www.ties.k12.mn.us/~mayatch/mq96/lesson/Heiroglyph/

Lesson Plans/Classroom Activities for Hieroglyphics Themes, from MayaQuest, presents teachers of middle school students with a variety of lesson plans for teaching about hieroglyphics.

Mr. Donn's Ancient History Lesson Plans and Activities

http://members.aol.com/DonnandLee/index.html

Mr. Donn's Ancient History Lesson Plans and Activities was developed by Don Donn, a middle school teacher from Maryland. The site features detailed units, lesson plans, and activities for Early Man, Mesopotamia, Egypt, Greece, Rome, China, Japan, India, Africa, Aztecs, Mayans, Incas and Middle Ages.

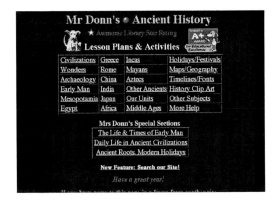

Social Studies Lesson Plans

Mr. Donn's U.S. History Lesson Plans and Activities

http://members.aol.com/donnandlee/
SiteIndex.html

Mr. Donn's U.S. History Lesson Plans and Activities (K-12) contains units, plans, activities, and resources for teaching about Native Americans, Colonial Period & Revolution, Western Expansion, Civil War, Modern America Emerges, 20th Century, and much more.

National Geographic Geography Lessons and Activities

www.nationalgeographic.com/resources/ngo/
education/ideas.html

National Geographic Geography Lessons and Activities provides lessons, units, and activities designed to bring good geography into the classroom. Click Kindergarten-4th Grade, 5th-8th Grade, and 9th-12th Grade to find the lesson plans and activities of your choice.

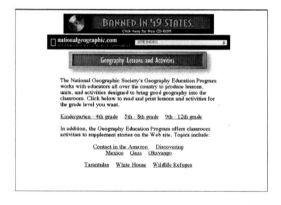

New Deal Network Classroom Lesson Plans

http://newdeal.feri.org/

New Deal Network Classroom Lesson Plans provides innovative ideas for classroom exercises, student projects, and additional sources of information about FDR and the New Deal. Titles of four of the lesson plans are TVA: Electricity for All, Dear Mrs. Roosevelt, Debating the FDR Memorial, and Rondal Partridge, NYA Photographer.

Nystromnet Geography Lesson Plans and Teaching Tips

www.nystromnet.com/lessonsandtips.html

Nystromnet Geography Lesson Plans and Teaching Tips contains quizzes; lesson plans for the primary, intermediate and high school levels; geography literacy games; and links to additional lessons in cyberspace.

Primary Sources and Activities

www.nara.gov/education/teaching/
teaching.html

Primary Sources and Activities provides secondary school teachers with reproducible primary documents from the holdings of the National Archives of the United States, with accompanying lesson plans correlated to the National History Standards. Among the many lesson plans are (1) Jackie Robinson: Beyond the Playing Field, (2) The Zimmermann Telegram, 1917, (3) Constitutional Issues: Separation of Powers—Franklin D. Roosevelt's attempt to increase the number of Justices on the Supreme Court—and (4) Constitutional Issues: Watergate and the Constitution. Additional links to primary source documents are also included.

160   *The Best Web Sites for Teachers*

Social Studies Lesson Plans

www.uiowa.edu/~socialed/pages/lessons.htm

Social Studies Lesson Plans were developed by students and faculty of the University of Iowa College of Education for Grades 9–12. The plans are organized in terms of the ten themes devised by the National Council for the Social Studies. Each plan consists of purpose, goals, materials, procedures, assessment, extensions, and resources.

South Carolina: Lessons From the Holocaust

www.scetv.org/HolocaustForum

South Carolina: Lessons From the Holocaust features 11 lesson plans, 34 student handouts, two series of taped interviews, a bibliography, and related sites to other curriculum resources.

Terry Jordan's Advanced Placement United States History Page

www.orangeschools.org/ohs/teachers/TJordan/Pages/index.html

Terry Jordan's Advanced Placement United States History Page offers teachers a syllabus for teaching advanced placement U.S. History. Also provided at the site are additional topics including: Lesson Plans, United States History for Grade 8, Projects, an A.P. U.S. History Chat Room, Weekly Reading Assignments, and Sample Unit Test Questions.

The Civil War Taught by a Soldier Who Was There

http://ole.net/ole/1996/lessons/middle/civil/civil.htm

The Civil War Taught by a Soldier Who Was There provides an Internet lesson from the editors of Online Educator. The next time you're teaching a unit on the American Civil War, the Internet can deliver a Civil War soldier to your school. His name is Newton Robert Scott, who served three years as a private in the Iowa Volunteers during the Civil War. Scott died more than 60 years ago, but his war correspondence lives on in cyberspace. Suggestions are given for many site-based interdisciplinary activities you can create for your students.

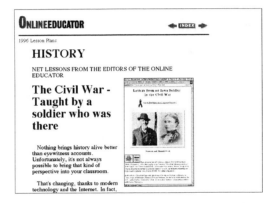

U.S. Government Lesson Plans

www.fred.net/nhhs/lessons/usg.htm

U.S. Government Lesson Plans, prepared by George Cassutto, a high school teacher, features 18 weeks of lesson plans and activities that teachers can adapt to U.S. government and other social studies classes.

What Do Maps Show?

http://info.er.usgs.gov/education/teacher/
what-do-maps-show/index.html

What Do Maps Show? offers lesson plans for four geography and map-reading lessons suitable for upper elementary and junior high school levels. Each lesson contains step-by-step procedures, hands-on student activity sheets, and reproducible maps. There is also a List of Materials link, which contains maps useful for teaching geography.

World Wise Schools

www.peacecorps.gov/www/dp/wws1.html

World Wise Schools, from the Peace Corps, provides a collection of global education lesson plans for social studies and other subjects indexed by Grade levels 3–12.

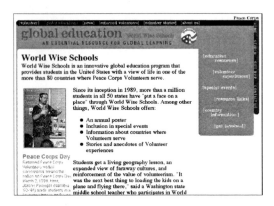

Abraham Lincoln Classroom Activities

www.siec.k12.in.us/~west/proj/lincoln/class.htm

Abraham Lincoln Classroom Activities was created by Tammy Payton's first-grade class. The site, suitable for the primary grades, includes an online quiz, an animation that shows the addition of states to the United States, a picture gallery of President Lincoln, a treasure hunt, suggestions for further classroom activities, and additional links.

Abraham Lincoln's Assassination

http://members.aol.com/RVSNorton/Lincoln.html

Abraham Lincoln's Assassination, a site organized by a U.S. history teacher, is appropriate for students in Grades 6-12. The site features links to Ford's Theatre, the Mary Surratt House Museum, reproductions of newspapers reporting the assassination of Lincoln in 1865, Dr. Mudd, the life of John Wilkes Booth, and other interesting facts about Lincoln's assassination.

Advanced Placement Program

www.collegeboard.org/ap/indx002.html

Advanced Placement Program, provided by College Board Online, features tips for teachers and students, information about A.P. classes and exams, and related Web sites for all A.P. subjects including economics, European and U.S. history, U.S. and comparative government, and psychology.

Adventure Online

www.adventureonline.com/about.html

Adventure Online for Grades 3-9, delivers Web-based, core learning materials in math, reading and writing, social studies, and science. Each lesson or activity is brought to life through a real-world adventure. Affordable, year-long subscriptions to teachers and students featuring lesson plans and activities are offered. Also available is a free sample adventure.

Africa Online for Kids Only

www.africaonline.com/AfricaOnline/coverkids.html

Africa Online for Kids Only is a site where elementary and middle school students can read a Kenyan magazine written for kids, play games and decode messages, learn about the more than 1,000 languages in Africa, meet African students online, find a keypal, or just browse around.

African American History

www.msstate.edu/Archives/History/USA/Afro-Amer/afro.html

African American History links to material on museums, newspapers, events, and people in black history, as well as numerous related links that celebrate the African American experience.

The American Civil War Homepage

http://sunsite.utk.edu/civil-war/

The American Civil War Homepage contains general resources, graphic images, letters, diaries, and links to other reference sites.

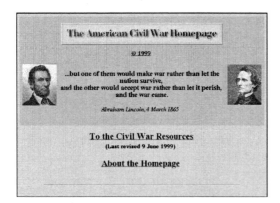

American Memory

http://rs6.loc.gov/amhome.html

American Memory, drawn mainly from the special collections of the Library of Congress, has direct links to photographic, recorded sounds, manuscript, and early motion picture collections.

The American Presidency

www.grolier.com/presidents/preshome.html

The American Presidency, from Grolier Online, presents an exclusive history of presidents, the presidency, politics, and related subjects. The site includes encyclopedias, sound bytes, flip cards, and presidential quizzes. It is suitable for Grades 6-12.

The American West

www.americanwest.com/

The American West focuses on the "old West" and includes information on cowboys, Native Americans, pioneers and pioneer towns, explorers, and more.

American Treasures of the Library of Congress

http://lcweb.loc.gov/exhibits/treasures/

American Treasures of the Library of Congress categorizes as "treasures" some of the more than 110 million items in the Library of Congress. These include Thomas Jefferson's handwritten draft of the Declaration of Independence, Jelly Roll Morton's early compositions, Maya Lin's original drawing for the Vietnam Veterans Memorial, the earliest known baseball cards, and the first motion picture deposited for copyright.

Anthropology on the Internet for K-12

www.sil.si.edu/SILPublications/Anthropology-K12/

Anthropology on the Internet for K-12 is a product of the Smithsonian Institution. It is an annotated listing of hot links to selected sites with information about the field of anthropology for teachers and young people. The sites are grouped under 11 different sections (including careers).

Architecture Through the Ages

http://library.advanced.org/10098

Architecture Through the Ages allows Middle school students to learn about architecture from the great Maya to the building of cathedrals.

Biographical Dictionary

www.s9.com/biography/

Biographical Dictionary, maintained by Eric Tentarelli, is an online dictionary that provides biographical information for more than 27,000 people from ancient times to the present day. It contains a searchable database and ideas for students and teachers on how to use the biographical dictionary as a classroom resource.

Black History: Exploring African-American Issues on the Web

www.kn.pacbell.com/wired/BHM/AfroAm.html

Black History: Exploring African-American Issues on the Web was created by Pacific Bell Knowledge Network Explorer and provides a wide variety of Internet-based resources that individual students or whole classes can use.

Blue Web'n Learning Applications

www.kn.pacbell.com/wired/bluewebn/

Blue Web'n Learning Applications, provided by Pacific Bell, includes lessons, activities, projects, resources, references, and tools for the K-12 teacher. Scroll to Content Table to find the History & Social Studies materials.

Capitals of the United States

www.awl.com/sf-aw/sfaw/resources/
statescapitals/

Capitals of the United States, provided by Scott Foresman, uses a game-like format for finding facts about the states and their capitals.

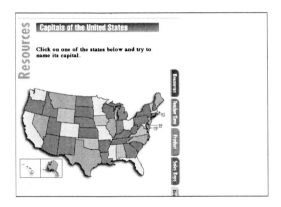

Celebrating the Life of Martin Luther King, Jr.

www.eduplace.com/ss/king/mlk.html

Celebrating the Life of Martin Luther King, Jr., from Houghton Mifflin, features activities and projects to help students of all ages explore the life and times of Dr. King. The site also includes links to other relevant resources.

Chinese Historical and Cultural Project

www.chcp.org/

Chinese Historical and Cultural Project based in Santa Clara County, California, promotes and preserves Chinese and Chinese-American history and culture through community outreach activities. The site includes a calendar of events, links to curriculum projects, and historic photographs.

CIA World Fact Book 1998

www.odci.gov/cia/publications/factbook/

CIA World Fact Book 1998 is a compilation of data about countries throughout the world.

CIA's Homepage for Kids

www.odci.gov/cia/ciakids/index.html

CIA's Homepage for Kids features history and geography resources and activities just for kids as well as a World Fact Book, CIA Canine Corps and Aerial Photography Pigeons, and a link to Home Pages for Kids that have been developed at other U.S. government agencies.

Civil War Gazette

www.itdc.sbcss.k12.ca.us/curriculum/
civilwar.html

Civil War Gazette, a student online activity, was developed by Jim Evans of the Redlands (California) Unified School District. Teams are assigned the task of using the computer to research, write, and edit a single edition of a historical newspaper that focuses on a specific battle during the Civil War. The site features all of the Internet resources students need to complete the assignment.

Computers in the Social Studies Journal

www.cssjournal.com/journal/

Computers in the Social Studies (CSS) Journal is an electronic educational journal dedicated to the advancement of personal computers and related technology in K–12+ social studies classrooms.

Congressional Email Directory

www.webslingerz.com/jhoffman/
congress-email.html

Congressional Email Directory provides the e-mail addresses of U.S. senators and representatives. You can click the address and write your lawmaker a letter.

Create a Newspaper!

www.twingroves.district96.k12.il.us/
NewspaperProj/Newspaper.html

Create a Newspaper!, designed by two Illinois teachers, provides an online activity for creating a historical newspaper. The site includes student assignments and Internet resources.

Cybrary of the Holocaust

http://remember.org/

Cybrary of the Holocaust is a place where you can share in teaching and learning about the Holocaust. You can journey through the Holocaust by interactive map, take a virtual tour of Auschwitz, and read diaries and interviews that can be used as background in teaching about this tragic historical event.

Daily Almanacs

http://shoga.wwa.com/~mjm/almanac2.html

Daily Almanacs allows you to select any calendar date and get a list of birthdays and notable events.

Donner Online

www.kn.pacbell.com/wired/donner/index.html

Donner Online is a Web-based activity in which middle and high school students learn about a topic by collecting information, images, and insights from the Internet, and then "pasting" them into a multimedia Scrapbook (a HyperStudio stack or a Web page) to share with others.

Introduction | The Task | The Process | The Roles | Conclusion | HyperText Dictionary

Introduction

The plight of the Donner Party remains one of the most poignant episodes in the history of westward expansion during the 19th Century. "Donner Online" is a type of Web-based activity in which you learn about a topic by collecting information, images, and insights from the Internet, and then you "paste" them into a multimedia Scrapbook (a HyperStudio stack or a Web page) to share your learning with others.

Educational Standards and Curriculum Frameworks for Social Studies

http://putwest.boces.org/StSu/Social.html

Educational Standards and Curriculum Frameworks for Social Studies is an annotated list of Internet sites with K–12 educational standards and curriculum frameworks documents. It is maintained by Charles Hill and the Putnam Valley Schools in New York. The listings are by social studies organization and by state.

EduStock

http://tqd.advanced.org/3088/

EduStock is an educational Web page that can teach high school students what the stock market is and how it can work for them. It includes tutorials on the stock market and how to pick good stocks. The site also provides information on a select group of companies to help students start their research into what stock is going to make their fortunes. It also provides the only free real-time stock market simulation on the World Wide Web.

Egyptian Hieroglyphics

www.torstar.com/rom/egypt/

Egyptian Hieroglyphics, a site at which Torstar Electronic Publishing Ltd. has identified the Egyptian phonograms that are closest to the English alphabet, allows students to translate between hieroglyphs and English.

Exploring China: A Multimedia Scrapbook Activity

www.kn.pacbell.com/wired/China/scrapbook.html

Exploring China: A Multimedia Scrapbook Activity permits middle and high school students to surf the Internet links at the site to find pictures, text, maps, facts, quotes, or controversies that capture their exploration of China. Students save the text and images they find important to create a multimedia scrapbook.

Famous American Trials

www.law.umkc.edu/faculty/projects/FTrials/ftrials.htm

Famous American Trials was developed by Doug Linder of the University of Missouri-Kansas City Law School. The site, suitable for secondary school students, presents 12 famous trials including Leopold and Loeb Trial, Scopes "Monkey" Trial, Rosenberg Trial, Amistad Trials, Salem Witchcraft Trials, and Scottsboro Trials. Also included are links to other trial resources, a Constitutional Trivia Quiz, and Bill of Rights Golf.

Flints and Stones: Real Life in Prehistory

www.ncl.ac.uk/~nantiq/menu.html

Flints and Stones: Real Life in Prehistory welcomes middle school students to the world of the Late Stone Age hunter-gatherers. Students explore this online world led by the Shaman, the leader of the Stone Age people.

From Revolution to Reconstruction and What Happened Afterwards

http://grid.let.rug.nl/~welling/usa/revolution

From Revolution to Reconstruction and What Happened Afterwards is an interactive American history textbook from the Colonial period to the First World War. It contains links to original sources and articles prepared by a number of contributors. Students can read the text sequentially or just go off on their own.

Historic Audio Archives

www.webcorp.com/sounds/index.htm

Historic Audio Archives is a collection of sound clips from the past. It includes the voices of Senator Joseph McCarthy, President Richard Nixon, leaders in the Civil Rights movement, and others.

The History Channel

www.historychannel.com/class/

The History Channel shows ways to make television programs from the History Channel exciting and useful in the social studies curriculum. The site contains program scheduling information and a weekly History Channel Quiz.

HyperHistory Online

www.hyperhistory.com/online_n2/History_n2/a.html

HyperHistory Online includes more than 3,000 facts related to science, culture, religion, and politics. The site, appropriate for students in Grades 7-12, also includes hundreds of color-coded lifelines of important persons and timelines for the major civilizations, accompanied by historical maps.

IBM Internet Lesson Plans

www.solutions.ibm.com/k12/teacher/lp_text.html

IBM Internet Lesson Plans features lesson plans and activities that encourage students in Grades 3-12 to use the Internet to do research. Plans have been provided for many curricular areas, including social studies. The site is updated monthly. An archive of previous Internet activities is provided.

KidsClick!

http://sunsite.berkeley.edu/KidsClick!/midhist.html

KidsClick! features resources to enrich several social studies areas, including Archaeology, Prehistoric People, Ancient World, Ancient Egypt, Greece and Rome, The Vikings, Middle Ages, Knights, Renaissance, Exploration, Pirates, American History (General), Revolutionary War, Civil War, Cowboys & the American West, World War I and II, and the Holocaust.

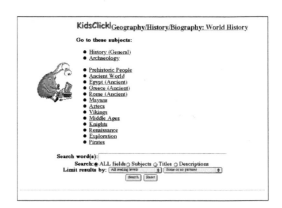

Little-Known Historical Facts

http://oneida-nation.net/facts/index.html

Little-Known Historical Facts features brief stories about Native American contributions in U.S. history. The site is suitable for Grades 4-8 and includes the Polly Cooper Story, the Battle of Oriskiny, Notes From the Past, and the Two-Row Wampum.

Living Africa

http://library.advanced.org/16645/
contents.html

Living Africa features the people, the land, wildlife, and national parks. Also included are a wildlife conservation game, virtual postcards, a virtual safari, an atlas, a quiz, a search engine, and links to other sites.

http://library.thinkquest.org/16645/contents.html

Martin Luther King, Jr.

http://webster.seatimes.com/mlk/index.html

Martin Luther King, Jr., is a site sponsored by the *Seattle Times*. You can find out about the man, the movement, and the legacy by going to an electronic classroom that features an interactive quiz and a study guide suitable for teachers and kids.

Middle Ages What Was It Really Like to Live in the Middle Ages?

www.learner.org/exhibits/middleages/

Middle Ages What Was It Really Like to Live in the Middle Ages? is inspired by programs from The Western Tradition, a video series in the Annenberg/CPB Multimedia Collection. Middle and high school students can find information about religion, homes, clothing, health, arts and entertainment, town life, and related resources.

Name That Flag!

www.futcher.com/nameflag/

Name That Flag! is a geography contest suitable for Grades 4–12. Students try to identify the country or origin of a flag and then enter their answers on an online form. A new flag is displayed after the current one is correctly identified. Names and home pages of winning entries are posted.

National Council for the Social Studies Online

www.ncss.org/

National Council for the Social Studies (NCSS) Online is the site of the professional organization representing social studies teachers in the United States. It is a showcase of teaching resources, professional development activities, publications, news, and Internet resources. It includes information on subscribing to a listserv for sharing ideas with other social studies teachers by e-mail.

NetSERF—Internet Connection for Medieval Resources

http://itassrva.cpit.cua.edu/netserf/

NetSERF—Internet Connection for Medieval Resources features links to resources on medieval art, architecture, history, law, music, and religion. The site also includes a research center.

Newsmaker Bios

http://abcnews.go.com/reference/bios/

Newsmaker Bios is part of the ABC News Web site that provides teachers and students with background material and information on the personalities making news around the world. The site features brief sketches that introduce world leaders and figures. For each person, users will find photographs, birthdate and -place, and education, along with quotes from and about the person.

NIE Online: Newspapers in Education

http://detnews.com/nie/index.html

NIE Online: Newspapers in Education, hosted by the *Detroit News*, provides online newspaper articles of interest to students in Grades 5–12. Articles are accompanied by discussion questions and links to other relevant Web sites. An archive of previous articles is also included.

The 1920s

http://homer.louisville.edu/~kprayb01/1920s.html

The 1920s, developed by Kevin Rayburn, features information about the Roaring '20s. It presents a '20s Timeline, People and Trends, and music of the era.

Odyssey in Egypt

www.website1.com/odyssey/

Odyssey in Egypt, developed by WebSiteOne and the Scriptorium Center for Christian Antiquities, was an interactive archaeological dig for middle school students. The site managers created, managed, transmitted, and served up pictures and text from Egypt on a weekly basis. Even though the project is no longer live, the information here can help history and geography teachers create interesting lessons.

Online Educator

http://ole.net/ole/index.shtml

Online Educator helps make the Internet an accessible, useful classroom tool. It includes super sites for teachers, search and browse features for lesson ideas in specific subjects, and a discussion forum.

The Oregon Trail

www.isu.edu/~trinmich/Oregontrail.html

The Oregon Trail is an online version of the award-winning documentary film aired nationally over PBS stations. It provides information, unusual facts, historic sites along the Oregon Trail, and a free teacher's guide containing classroom activities.

Perry-Castañeda Library Map Collection

www.lib.utexas.edu/Libs/PCL/Map_collection/Map_collection.html

Perry-Castañeda Library Map Collection was prepared by the University of Texas at Austin. It contains electronic maps of current and general interest for many regions of the world.

School Projects That Connect with the Internet

www.siec.k12.in.us/~west/proj

School Projects That Connect with the Internet provides links to projects developed by Loogootee Elementary West teachers for children in Grades K-3 (ages 5-9).

SCORE History-Social Science Resources

http://score.rims.k12.ca.us/

SCORE History-Social Science Resources is part of the Network of Online Resource Centers in California linking quality resources from the World Wide Web to the California curriculum (K-12). The site includes resources that involve kids in online activities. Suggested activities for effective use of the resources with students are included, as well as a search engine that allows you to search by grade level or by theme/topic.

Searching for China WebQuest

www.kn.pacbell.com/wired/China/ChinaQuest.html

Searching for China WebQuest is sponsored by Pacific Bell Knowledge Network. It allows your students to join a team and take on a role (foreign investor, human rights worker, museum curator, California state senator, or religious leader). The team members work together to create a special report that makes sense of the complex country that is China. The site also includes a Teacher's Guide.

Social Studies Center

www.eduplace.com/ss/

Social Studies Center, from Houghton Mifflin and appropriate for Grades 4-8, features online games, interactive quizzes, information on current events, and online maps for students. Teachers will find classroom activities, professional resources, and links to other relevant social studies materials.

Social Studies School Service

www.socialstudies.com/

Social Studies School Service has long been a leader in educational supplementary materials for the social studies. The organization now presents teachers with an online catalog, free teachers' guides, and links to other Web sites. Select the What's New button for a monthly feature focusing on an important social studies theme. Lesson plans and student exercises are included.

The Spanish-American War in Motion Pictures

http://lcweb2.loc.gov/ammem/sawhtml/sawhome.html

The Spanish-American War in Motion Pictures, sponsored by the Library of Congress, presents films of the Spanish-American War and the Philippine Insurrection produced between 1898 and 1901. The films are displayed in QuickTime, .mpg, and .avi formats.

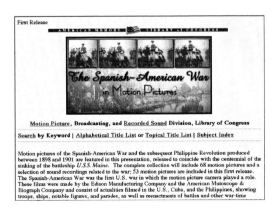

Supreme Court Collection

http://supct.law.cornell.edu/supct/

Supreme Court Collection, sponsored by LII Legal Information Institute, contains information on recent decisions of the U.S. Supreme Court. The site also includes selected pre-1990 decisions, a gallery of the justices, and information on how to subscribe by e-mail to receive U.S. Supreme Court decisions only hours after their release.

Teaching Current Events Via Newspapers, Magazines and TV

www.csun.edu/~hcedu013/cevents.html

Teaching Current Events Via Newspapers, Magazines and TV offers teachers lesson plans, activities, and resources for making current events more productive and interesting in the K–12 classroom.

Teen Court TV

www.courttv.com/teens/

Teen Court TV (from the Court TV channel) is designed to give teenagers an inside look at the justice system. The program consists of three shows, including What's the Verdict?, a one-hour show that invites teenagers to analyze real trials just as jurors do. Cases are picked that have already reached a conclusion, and the guests get to compare their verdicts to the ones actually reached in court. What's the Verdict airs on Saturday and on Sunday at 1:00 p.m. All times are Eastern.

Time for Kids

www.pathfinder.com/TFK/

Time for Kids, for Grades 2-6, features information on people and events in the news, historic profiles, a cartoon of the week, interactive talk, and online quizzes.

U.S. Census Bureau

www.census.gov/

U.S. **Census Bureau** is a site that includes data maps, interactive software to view profiles of states and countries, and economic information. You can e-mail your questions and comments to the Ask-the-Experts page, search the census bureau database, and subscribe to a mailing list.

U.S. House of Representatives

www.house.gov/

U.S. **House of Representatives** home page provides public access to legislative information as well as information about members, committees, and organizations of the House. The site includes links to other U.S. government information resources.

United States Senate

www.senate.gov/

The **United States Senate** is a site that provides information about the members of the Senate, Senate committees, and Senate leadership and support offices. It also includes general background information about U.S. Senate legislative procedures, Senate facilities in the Capitol Building, and the history of the Senate.

The Valley of the Shadow: Living the Civil War in Pennsylvania and Virginia

http://jefferson.village.virginia.edu/vshadow/vshadow.html

The Valley of the Shadow: Living the Civil War in Pennsylvania and Virginia interweaves the histories of two communities on either side of the Mason-Dixon line during the American Civil War. The site, appropriate for Grades 8-12, features pages from newspapers of the time, original census returns, diaries and maps, selected army rosters, photos, and commentary.

Vietnam: Yesterday and Today

www.oakton.edu/~wittman/

Vietnam: Yesterday and Today, prepared by Sandra M. Wittman, provides a chronology of the war and materials for study and teaching. It also has links to other relevant Web resources.

Watergate

http://vcepolitics.com/wgate/intro.htm

Watergate, assembled by Malcolm Farnsworth, a teacher, is a large body of information about the Watergate scandal. The site includes a chronology of events and numerous links to speeches and background information. The site is appropriate for secondary school students.

Weekly Reader Galaxy

www.weeklyreader.com/

Weekly Reader Galaxy, an online newspaper provided by the Weekly Reader Corporation, features social studies activities for students in Grades K-6. These include news, polls, contests, games, and mystery photos.

Women in World History Curriculum

http://home.earthlink.net/~womenwhist/

Women in World History Curriculum, directed by Lyn Reese, is an interactive site full of information and resources about women's experiences in world history. It includes female heroes, lesson plans, reviews of classroom materials, and links to other resources.

World Surfari

www.supersurf.com/

World Surfari allows elementary and middle school students to take a virtual "surfari" to a different country every month! The site is produced by Brian Giacoppo, now age 13.

The World War I Document Archive

www.lib.byu.edu/~rdh/wwi/

The World War I Document Archive, assembled by volunteers of the World War I Military History List, allows users to locate primary documents concerning the Great War. Documents are organized by year: pre-1914 through post-1918. Also included are memorials and personal reminiscences, a W.W. I biographical dictionary, an image archive, and links to other relevant W.W. I sites.

World War I: Trenches on the Web

www.worldwar1.com/

World War I: Trenches on the Web features information on people, places, and events that led to one of the tragic episodes in modern history. The site also includes a poster collection and reference resources.

World War II Commemoration

http://gi.grolier.com/wwii/

World War II Commemoration, presented by Grolier Online, features the story of World War II, biographies and articles, air combat films, photographs, a World War II history test, and World War II links.

Abraham Lincoln Online

www.netins.net/showcase/creative/lincoln.html

Abraham Lincoln Online presents historic Lincoln sites, resources, pictures, speeches, and writings, as well as a Lincoln Quiz-of-the-Month. You can also add your views to an online discussion.

AFRO-Americ@'s Black History Museum

www.afroam.org/history/history.html

AFRO-Americ@'s Black History Museum, sponsored by AT&T, presents interactive exhibits appropriate for Grades 8-12. Topics include Black Resistance-Slavery in the U.S., Tuskegee Airmen, Jackie Robinson, Black Panther Party, Black or White, Million Man March, Scottsboro Boys, and This Is Our War.

The Ancient Olympic Games Virtual Museum

http://devlab.dartmouth.edu/olympic/

The Ancient Olympic Games Virtual Museum provides a plethora of information about these contests, the forefathers of our modern Olympic Games. The online museum includes a tour of the site, the story of a competitor, descriptions of the ancient events, a slide show of modern Greece, and related Web sites.

Benjamin Franklin: Glimpses of the Man

http://sln.fi.edu/franklin/rotten.html

Benjamin Franklin: Glimpses of the Man takes you to the Franklin Institute's online exhibit on this multitalented Founding Father.

Colonial Lexington

http://hastings.ci.lexington.ma.us/WebPages/Colonial/Colonial.html

Colonial Lexington was begun by students at the Maria Hastings School in Lexington, Massachusetts. The site, suitable for middle school kids, includes links to information on the battle, colonial life and crafts, important people and families, historic homes, Paul Revere's Ride, and more.

Colonial Williamsburg

www.history.org/

Colonial Williamsburg features information on the life and times of Colonial America. The site also includes a Colonial dateline highlighting events from 1750 to 1783. It also has resources for teachers and students in Grades 5-12.

1492: An Ongoing Voyage

http://sunsite.unc.edu/expo/1492.exhibit/Intro.html

1492: An Ongoing Voyage is a Library of Congress exhibit of photos and discussions about Columbus' discovery of America.

George Washington's Mount Vernon Estate and Gardens

www.mountvernon.org/

George Washington's Mount Vernon Estate and Gardens provides a tour of our first President's home, library, and grounds. The site also includes links to additional resources.

Japanese American Internment, Santa Clara Valley

http://scuish.scu.edu/SCU/Programs/
Diversity/exhibit1.html

Japanese American Internment, Santa Clara Valley is on permanent display at the Japanese American Resource Center in San Jose, California's Japantown. The online exhibit depicts the internment camp life of the many local Santa Clara Valley Japanese Americans who were interned.

The Library of Congress Exhibitions

http://marvel.loc.gov/

The Library of Congress Exhibitions lists exhibits, events, and services and provides information on how to use their online library for your own research.

Monticello: The Home of Thomas Jefferson

www.monticello.org/

Monticello: The Home of Thomas Jefferson allows you to follow Jefferson through his day and to use a clickable index to find information on a variety of matters relating to the third U.S. president.

Old Sturbridge Village

www.osv.org/

Old Sturbridge Village takes you back in time and lets you visit the largest historical museum in the Northeast. The museum, located in Sturbridge, Massachusetts, re-creates the daily work activities and community celebrations of a rural 19th-century town.

Pyramids—The Inside Story

www.pbs.org/wgbh/pages/nova/pyramid/

Pyramids—The Inside Story is sponsored by Nova Online. Students can wander through the chambers and passageways of the Great Pyramid, and learn about the pharaohs for whom these monumental tombs were built.

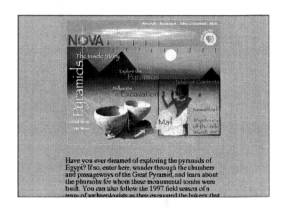

The Spanish Missions of California

http://ananke.advanced.org/3615/

The Spanish Missions of California is a place where teachers and students can find out who created the missions and why, take a tour of a typical mission, and learn about the people who lived there. Included is a page just for teachers and links to more places to find additional information.

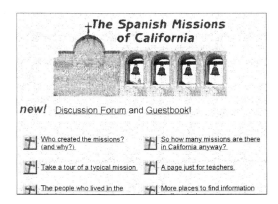

United States Holocaust Memorial Museum Online Exhibitions

www.ushmm.org/exhibits/exhibit.htm

United States Holocaust Memorial Museum Online Exhibitions provides high school teachers and students with a series of online exhibitions relating to the history of the Holocaust.

Walking Tour of Plimoth Plantation

http://spirit.lib.uconn.edu/ArchNet/Topical/Historic/Plimoth/Plimoth.html

Walking Tour of Plimoth Plantation provides images and descriptions of the first permanent European settlement in southern New England, dating from 1620.

Welcome to the White House

www.whitehouse.gov/

Welcome to the White House offers a tour of our president's home. You can listen to speeches, view photos, search White House documents, and e-mail the president and vice-president.

White House for Kids

www.whitehouse.gov/WH/kids/html/home.html

White House for Kids introduces Socks, the first cat, who leads kids on a tour of the White House. They can learn about its history and about other kids and pets who have lived there, as well as send e-mail to the president, vice-president, and first lady.

Special Education

British Columbia Ministry of Education—Special Education On-line Documents

www.bced.gov.bc.ca/specialed/docs.htm

British Columbia Ministry of Education—Special Education On-line Documents provides teachers with resources and teaching tips for working with special education students. Resources are available for teaching the visually impaired, those with a hearing loss, the intellectually disabled, the gifted, and students with a variety of chronic health conditions ranging from allergies to spina bifida.

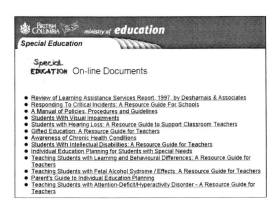

Special Education Lesson Plans

www.geocities.com/Athens/Forum/6727/lessons.html

Special Education Lesson Plans provides 20 primary and 16 intermediate unit plans developed by teachers from four elementary schools in Kansas City and Burlington, Kansas, as an outgrowth of a project to include students with special education needs in their classrooms. Each unit is structured in a similar manner consisting of specific outcomes and objectives, activities, and followed by team planning pages.

The Arc Home Page

http://TheArc.org/welcome.html

The Arc Home Page, sponsored by the country's largest voluntary organization committed to the welfare of all children and adults with mental retardation, provides links to sites of interest to teachers and parents.

Blind Childrens Center

www.blindcntr.org/bcc/

Blind Childrens Center is a nonprofit organization available to blind and partially sighted children. The site provides information about educational preschool programs, social services, infant stimulation programs, and support and volunteer opportunities. Also provided are links to other relevant resources.

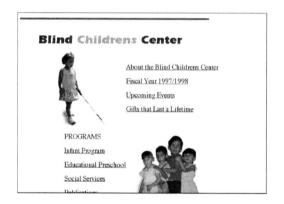

California's School-to-Work Interagency Transition Partnership

www.sna.com/switp/

California's School-to-Work Interagency Transition Partnership (SWITP) is a statewide effort to help students with disabilities to move successfully from school to work. The site provides links to information about employment and training resources, people who can provide technical assistance, information for parents and consumers, and links to additional resources.

Center for the Study of Autism

www.autism.org/

Center for the Study of Autism (CSA) provides information about autism to parents and professionals and includes several links to relevant resources for teachers.

Children and Adults with Attention Deficit Disorders

www.chadd.org/

Children and Adults With Attention Deficit Disorders (CH.A.D.D.) is a nonprofit, parent-based organization formed to better the lives of individuals with attention deficit disorders. The site provides links to resources for parenting, teaching, and treating kids who have this disability.

Children with Special Needs

http://dent.edmonds.wednet.edu/IMD/specialchild.html

Children with Special Needs is produced by Edmonds (Washington) School District. It provides links to a variety of special needs (K-12) from ADD to the visually impaired and includes a medical search engine. The site also provides information about computer adaptive software and wheelchairs.

Deaf World Web

http://dww.deafworldweb.org/

Deaf World Web features links to Web resources in 36 countries of the world. The menu also includes a search tool for finding additional information about deaf culture, as well as a Discussion Forum. A French version is also available.

Early Childhood Thematic Units

www.sbcss.k12.ca.us/sbcss/specialeducation/ecthematic/

Early Childhood Thematic Units, appropriate for special education, incorporate technology throughout. They include ideas for bulletin boards, cooking, literature, fine and gross motor activities, language development, music, toys and materials, and software. Although most suitable for the preschool level, they can also be a source of ideas for teachers working with primary pupils. Some of the units are: The Zoo, At the Farm, Halloween, Thanksgiving/Foods, Transportation, and Insects.

Family Village: A Global Community of Disability-Related Resources

www.familyvillage.wisc.edu/index.htmlx

Family Village: A Global Community of Disability-Related Resources is a directory of resources covering disability issues on the Internet. It also provides a set of discussion lists and chat rooms.

Gifted Resources Home Page

www.eskimo.com/~user/kids.html

Gifted Resources Home Page contains links to all known online gifted resources, enrichment programs, talent searches, summer programs, mailing lists, and early acceptance programs. More resources will be added as they become available.

Internet Resources for Special Children (IRSC)

www.irsc.org/

Internet Resources for Special Children (IRSC) offers valuable information for parents, family members, caregivers, friends, educators, and medical professionals who interact with children who have disabilities. Provided are disability links, a search engine, and articles from local newspapers and school districts as well as those written by online media columnists.

LD OnLine

www.ldonline.org/index.html

LD OnLine is an interactive guide to learning disabilities for parents, teachers, and children. The site highlights new information in the field of learning disabilities, has information on every aspect of learning disabilities, features a comprehensive listing of learning disabilities events on the Internet, offers personal essays on first-hand experiences with the challenges of learning disabilities and audio clips from experts in the field, and provides bulletin boards, a chat room, an LD store, and an online newsletter.

The National Federation of the Blind

www.nfb.org/

The National Federation of the Blind (NFB) is the largest organization of the blind in America. There are links to Braille literacy, government and community services, legislation, research, and technology.

Outside the Box

http://home.att.net/~adhd.kids/

Outside the Box, produced by Laurie Shagberg, is a place for parents and teachers who recognize the special needs of kids who have ADHD (Attention Deficit Disorder) and/or Learning Disabilities, who are gifted but who struggle, and who don't exactly fit inside the box of the classroom. The site contains articles, discussion lists, links to a variety of resources, and good advice.

Sign Writing Site

www.SignWriting.org/

Sign Writing Site provides sign-writing lessons as well as an online American Sign Language picture dictionary. The site also includes online versions of *Cinderella—Part One, Cinderella—Part Two, Humpty Dumpty*, and *Goldilocks and the Three Bears* written in English and American Sign Language for Grades K-12.

Special Educator's Web Pages

www.geocities.com/Athens/Styx/7315/

Special Educator's Web Pages produced by Kay Smith of the Clark County (Nevada) schools, contains information useful to K-12 teachers, including lesson planning; grants; behavior management; research; statutes, regulations, and case law; and free materials.

Special Needs Education

www.schoolnet.ca/sne/

Special Needs Education (SNE) endeavors to maintain a comprehensive and current Web directory of resources relating to special education. Select resources for a directory of specific disability topics, including Dyslexia, Attention Deficit Disorder, Down Syndrome, and Gifted Education. For lesson plans, diagnostic tools, and other teaching and learning information, visit the teacher and parent resource area.

Special Needs Resources

www.bushnet.qld.edu.au/~sarah/spec_ed/

Special Needs Resources is designed for teachers and parents interested in special education. Resources feature Arts and Crafts, Cooking, and Theme Ideas. The site also includes software reviews, links to sites in the areas of special needs and technology, and an articles section.

Teaching Ideas for Early Childhood Special Educators

www.mcps.k12.md.us/curriculum/pep/teach.htm

Teaching Ideas for Early Childhood Special Educators groups ideas according to themes. Also provided are a database of teaching ideas and links to other resources.

Vocational/ Technical Education

Business Education Lesson Plans and Resources

www.angelfire.com/ks/tonyaskinner/index.html

Business Education Lesson Plans and Resources contains plans and resources for Accounting, Business Law, Computers, Economics, General Business, Internet, Keyboarding, and Office Tech. There are also links to professional organizations and a job search section.

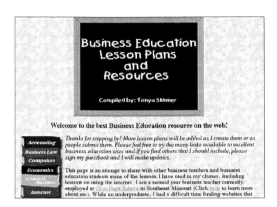

Computer Skills Lesson Plans

www.dpi.state.nc.us/Curriculum/
Computer.skills/lssnplns/CompCurr.LP.html

Computer Skills Lesson Plans, provided by the North Carolina Department of Public Instruction, features a series of lesson plans to help North Carolina teachers implement the state's computer skills curriculum. There is at least one lesson for each measure in the computer skills curriculum, as well as links to other curriculum areas.

IBM Internet Lesson Plans

www.solutions.ibm.com/k12/teacher/
lp_text.html

IBM Internet Lesson Plans feature lesson plans and activities that encourage students in Grades 3-12 to use the Internet to do research. Plans are provided for a variety of curriculum areas.

Lesson Plans and Activities Technology

www.mcrel.org/resources/links/techlessons.asp

Lesson Plans and Activities Technology is provided by the Mid-continent Regional Educational Laboratory (McREL), a nonprofit organization dedicated to improving the quality of education for all students. The site features 41 plans and ideas for integrating technology and the Internet into the K-12 classroom.

Sample Internet Lesson Plans and Learning Projects

www.schoolnet.ca/aboriginal/lessons/

Sample Internet Lesson Plans and Learning Projects presents lesson plans developed by Abenaki Associates. The plans are designed to (1) teach something about the Internet, (2) teach how to use the Internet, and (3) teach something by using information gained from the Internet. Many of the lessons are adaptable to the age group of the students in your classroom. Other lessons will be more suitable for experienced Internet users.

Wired Learning in the Classroom & Library: Design Team Applications

www.kn.pacbell.com/wired/wiredApps.html

Wired Learning in the Classroom & Library: Design Team Applications, provided by Pacific Bell, features activities, projects, resources, and tools to infuse technology in the K-12 classroom.

America's Job Bank

www.ajb.dni.us

America's Job Bank links 1,800 state employment offices across the country and lists 250,000 jobs.

Community Learning Network

www.cln.org/cln.html

Community Learning Network is intended to help the K-12 teacher integrate the Internet into the classroom in all curriculum areas. Teachers and students can "Ask the Expert" specific questions and receive replies, get background information and teaching tips, and find links to Internet keypal exchanges and Internet projects.

Computers in Elementary Education

http://nimbus.temple.edu/~jallis00/

Computers in Elementary Education was designed by Jane Allison for the elementary school computer teacher, who may be called on to teach a computer class, maintain a computer lab, or provide guidance to other teachers. The site provides links to educational sites, lesson plans, and ideas for using computers in the K-8 curriculum.

Filamentality

www.kn.pacbell.com/wired/fil/

Filamentality is a fill-in-the-blank, interactive Web site that guides teachers through picking a topic, searching the Web, gathering good Internet sites, and turning Web resources into activities appropriate for students. Filamentality has tips and help pages to hold a teacher's hand through the process. Teachers can even use Filamentality if they're newcomers to the Web.

Florida School-to-Work Information Navigator

www.flstw.fsu.edu/

Florida School-to-Work Information Navigator provides a variety of school-to-work resources. You can find links to grants and legislation, organizations and contacts, and work/labor employment. You can also subscribe to a mailing list.

International Technology Education Association

www.iteawww.org/

International Technology Education Association (ITEA) contains a variety of information on technology education, including links to several states' technology Web sites. Click Resources and then K-12 Sites for links to elementary schools, middle schools, and high schools that have technology education home pages.

Job Options

www.joboptions.com/esp/plsql/
espan_enter.espan_home

Job Options features a job and employer search engine as well as facilities for creating and posting résumés online. The site makers also permit a student to sign up, and they'll search a jobs database and e-mail any new openings that match the student's interests.

Journal of Industrial Teacher Education

http://scholar.lib.vt.edu/ejournals/JITE/jite.html

Journal of Industrial Teacher Education is an online journal for vocational education teachers.

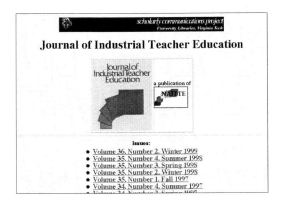

National Center for Research in Vocational Education

http://ncrve.berkeley.edu/

National Center for Research in Vocational Education (NCRVE), from the University of California, Berkeley, is the nation's largest center for research and development in work-related education. The site provides links to NCRVE publications, newsletters, and digests, as well as to other vocational education resources of interest to teachers and students.

New York State Education Department— Workforce Preparation and Continuing Education

www.nysed.gov/workforce/tabwork4.html

New York State Education Department— Workforce Preparation and Continuing Education provides vocational and technology education teachers with links to resources, including Curriculum and Teaching, School Improvement, and Journals and Organizations.

Technology Student Association

www.tsawww.org/

Technology Student Association (TSA) is an organization for elementary school, middle school, and high school students interested in technology education. It includes information on competitions, conferences, publications, and supplies, and offers links to other technology-related Web sites. Students can also view recent issues of *School Scene* published by TSA.

WWW 4 Teachers

www.4teachers.org/home/index.shtml

WWW 4 Teachers is designed for teachers powering learning with technology. There is a how-to information system on technology for educators; Web lessons ready-to-go; new ideas, activities, and resources by teachers; and a Kids Speak section where students tell what they are doing with technology in the classroom.

Appendix 1

Newsgroups
(USENET)
and Mailing Lists
(Listserv)

Deja News

www.deja.com/

Deja News is a search engine dedicated to Internet discussion newsgroups. Type in a specific question or topic and the search engine will find the date, newsgroup, subject, and the author. The search has four levels: standard, adult, complete, and jobs.

EdWeb

http://edweb.gsn.org/

EdWeb offers a collection of the best online educational resources available for K–12 students. These resources include newsgroups (public messages posted for everyone to see), listserv discussion groups (these are like private newsletters; you subscribe to a topic and then receive the latest news and views by e-mail), and electronic journals. To get to these groups, click Home Room at the bottom of the page, scroll down, and click Educational Resource Guide.

When you reach the EdWeb K–12 Resource Guide, click USENET News Group for lists of more than three dozen newsgroups for teachers and kids. The newsgroups focus on every subject in the K–12 curriculum, including art, business education, health and physical education, math, music, social studies, and many others. You can read what other teachers think and, if you wish, write messages of your own. You can click Listserv Discussion Groups and E-Journals to find a long list of education-centered private newsletters (mailing lists) to which you can subscribe. There is a mailing list for just about every topic of interest to K–12 educators.

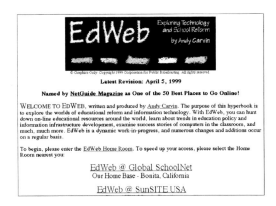

Appendix 2

Search Tools

All-in-One Search Page

www.allonesearch.com/

All-in-One Search Page features a compilation of various search tools to help you find things on the Internet. For example, scroll down the page and click World Wide Web. There, you will find AltaVista Web Search, InfoSeek, Lycos, WebCrawler, Yahoo, and other search tools. Just enter keywords, and your search of the Web begins. If you want to find tools to search for someone's e-mail address, return to the Home Page and click People. If you are interested in software, click Software to search for useful programs you can download. If you want to find USENET Newsgroups, click General Internet.

The Internet Sleuth

www.isleuth.com/

The Internet Sleuth provides you with quick keyword searches of more than 1,000 searchable databases on the Internet. Enter a keyword in Lycos, InfoSeek, AltaVista, Yahoo!, or Deja News to find lists of Internet sites that may contain the requested information. You can also search the Internet Sleuth by category, for example, Education, Math, or Science.

Inference Find

www.infind.com/

Inference Find is a fast search engine that eliminates duplicates while organizing results. Not only does it search across several search engines (AltaVista, Excite, InfoSeek, Lycos, WebCrawler, and Yahoo!), but it can also be configured to search any search engine.

Appendix 3

Evaluation Forms

Educational Web Sites Recommended by Others

Use this form to record and supplement information on educational Web sites described in this book or recommended to you by others. The form allows you to collect Web site information that is more detailed than the information you may have originally been given, and can be used to evaluate the site's usefulness in terms of your own particular needs.

Site Name: _____ Site Address/URL: _____

Brief Description: _____

_____

This site was recommended by: _____

For: _____

I could use this site for the following:
❏ Reference source for my students (appropriate reading level and content)
❏ Source of up-to-date data for analysis by my students
❏ Source of project(s) for my classes to join
❏ Source of connections to other projects at other sites
❏ Question/answer site where students can have their questions answered
❏ Ask-an-Expert sessions (special sessions to interact with a writer or other expert)
❏ Interactive sessions (students interact with the site's learning activity while online)
❏ Reference for myself (content for my subject area, lesson plans, etc.)
❏ Newsgroup site where I can share and get information
❏ Professional information site (educational research or other relevant material)
❏ Other: _____

Educational Setting—Mark all that apply: K 1 2 3 4 5 6 7 8 9 10 11 12 T
❏ Individual students   ❏ Downloadable content   ❏ Completely interactive
❏ Student groups   ❏ Interactive time necessary

Subject Areas—Check all that apply:
❏ Language Arts   ❏ Social Studies   ❏ Science
❏ Mathematics   ❏ Arts   ❏ Foreign Language
❏ Careers   ❏ Business   ❏ Cross-Curricular

Rate the site performance for each criterion listed.

	Exemplary	Adequate	Unacceptable
Content			
Does the content meet my needs?	❏	❏	❏
Educational Value			
Can students collaborate with other sites?	❏	❏	❏
Can teachers share results?	❏	❏	❏
Does the site respond to student questions?	❏	❏	❏
Technical Quality			
Is the site easy for my students to navigate?	❏	❏	❏
Overall Rating	❏	❏	❏

Educational Web Sites You Discover

Use this form to record complete information on educational Web sites you discover as you explore the World Wide Web. The information can be used to help you evaluate the site's usefulness in terms of your own particular needs.

Site Name: _____ Site Address/URL: _____

Brief Description: _____

_____

Approximate time necessary to access and download desired information: _____

Check all the categories that describe the site:

❏ Student Reference   ❏ Question/Answer   ❏ Newsgroup
❏ Data Source   ❏ Access to an Expert   ❏ Professional Information
❏ Student Projects   ❏ Interactive   ❏ Other _____
❏ Connections to Other Projects ❏ Teacher Reference

Educational Setting—Mark all that apply: K 1 2 3 4 5 6 7 8 9 10 11 12 T

❏ Individual students   ❏ Downloadable content   ❏ Completely interactive
❏ Student groups   ❏ Interactive time necessary

Subject Areas—Check all that apply:

❏ Language Arts   ❏ Social Studies   ❏ Science
❏ Mathematics   ❏ Arts   ❏ Foreign Language
❏ Careers   ❏ Business   ❏ Cross-Curricular

Rate the site performance for each criterion listed.

	Exemplary	Adequate	Unacceptable
Content			
1. Is it correct, accurate?	❏	❏	❏
2. Is it from an authoritative source?	❏	❏	❏
3. Is it free from stereotypes and bias?	❏	❏	❏
4. Is this the best medium for this information?	❏	❏	❏
5. Do the images enhance the content?	❏	❏	❏
Educational Value			
1. Is the information useful?	❏	❏	❏
2. Is the information readable by students?	❏	❏	❏
3. Is the information available elsewhere?	❏	❏	❏
4. Can students collaborate with other sites?	❏	❏	❏
5. Can teachers share results?	❏	❏	❏
6. Does the site respond to student questions?	❏	❏	❏
Technical Quality			
1. Does the site work the way it is intended to work?	❏	❏	❏
2. Are all the links current?	❏	❏	❏
3. Is the home page concise and quick to view?	❏	❏	❏
4. Are lengthy picture files saved for later pages?	❏	❏	❏
5. Is the menu clear, informative, and current?	❏	❏	❏
6. Is the navigation for the site obvious?	❏	❏	❏
Overall Rating	❏	❏	❏

Index